The Psychology
of the
Integral Society

The Psychology
of the
Integral Society

Michael Laitman, PhD
answers questions by
Anatloy Ulianov, PhD

LAITMAN
KABBALAH PUBLISHERS

The Psychology of the Integral Society

Published by Laitman Kabbalah Publishers
www.kabbalah.info   info@kabbalah.info
1057 Steeles Avenue West, Suite 532, Toronto, ON, M2R 3X1, Canada
2009 85th Street #51, Brooklyn, New York, 11214, USA

Printed in Canada

ISBN 978-1-897448-69-4
Library of Congress Control Number: 2011914225

Editors: E. Sotnikova, A. Posternak, T. Spivak, E. Hayman,
I. Popovich, A. Brener
Translation: Keren Applebaum
Copy Editor: Debra Rudder
Layout: Baruch Khovov
Cover: Inna Smirnova
Executive Editor: Chaim Ratz
Publishing and Post Production: Uri Laitman

FIRST EDITION: MAY 2012
First printing

CONTENTS

INTRODUCTION

The world we are living in today is global and integral.

This means that all of its components and systems are completely interdependent, and each element determines the fate of all the other elements in the world. This state is the result of progress, and from this moment on, there is no room for discord among the different parts of the world, since anything that is against integration is against progress, evolution, and most important, the law of Nature.

We all must realize that the absolute connection between all the parts of the world is a fact.

A person who goes along with this integration will succeed because *he will have the necessary skills for survival.*

Today, it is not the strongest individuals who will survive. Rather, survival depends upon one's ability to understand and appreciate that integration, cooperation, interconnection, mutual guarantee, concessions, and unification are Nature's call. The goal of Nature is to bring humanity to equivalence with Nature itself, to the ultimate harmony amongst all of its parts, and to complete perfection.

ABOUT THE AUTHORES

Anatoly Ulyanov is a Gestalt-therapist certified by the European Association for Gestalt Therapy (EAGT), a professor of Psychology at the Aesthetic Education Institute in Moscow, a trainer and instructor at the International Academy of Leadership in St. Petersburg, and a consultant for a variety of television programs.

Michael Laitman is a professor of Ontology and the Theory of Knowledge, a PhD in Philosophy and Kabbalah, and an MS in Bio-Cybernetics. He is the founder and president of the Ashlag Research Institute (ARI), a non-commercial organization that works to realize innovative ideas in educational politics for resolving systemic problems in modern education and upbringing. He has written over 40 books that have been translated into more than 17 languages.

NATURE'S CALL TO UNITY

- Children from Another World
- Creating a New, Unifying Internet
- The Revelation of the New World Is in Communication
- The Internet Above Physical Contact
- The Role of the Instructor in the Upbringing
- The Parents' Participation in Integral Upbringing
- A Method for Children and Adults
- A Differential, Integral Approach to Nature
- The Criterion for Success Is Man's Integrity in the Environment
- The Skill of Acting in Upbringing

CHILDREN FROM ANOTHER WORLD

It has been several months since we began our conversations on integral psychology, and during this time we have been trying to apply the method you describe. Based on this experience, I have some observations to present and some questions that I would like to pose to you today.

– As it turns out, children are far more ready to accept the method of integral psychology than their parents.

– And perhaps children are even more ready than the instructors themselves; children are ahead of everyone.

- Parents have to be prepared not only to ensure that they do not interfere with their children's development, but also to understand that this method will help them, as well. So what is the role of parents in this method?

- Today's children are completely different. We don't know the characteristics of the new world, so it seems to us that children today are strange and eccentric. Indeed, they really are not like us. They seem strange to us because they are born with preexisting rudiments of the next social state of the world, one that is global and integral, in accord with the challenge that Nature is presenting before us today. By pressuring us from within and from without, Nature is forcing us to adopt a new form of connection between us, for which we adults have no desire whatsoever.

Yet, today children are already born with a predisposition for integral perception, so while the new reality might seem strange to us, to them it is completely natural and even desirable. Children understand it so well that they might as well have come to us from another world, and weren't really our kids at all. They perceive everything as natural because the integral perception really is natural. It is the nature of reality that is gradually being revealed today.

Therefore, it's not the children who have a problem, it is the parents and teachers who are trying to implement a new method of connection among people, a method offered to them by Nature. The adults are still in a transition phase, while the children are already ripe for it.

Now is really a special time. We are in the midst of a transition from an egoistic, proprietary, individual level—where the relationships between us are self-serving—to an altruistic, integral, and global level, where everyone must be interconnected.

How can we make this transformation? Only with the help of mass media. This transformation will be possible if public representatives and the world's influential people understand the need for change, and take it on themselves to care for the future generation.

But as usual, everything falls on the shoulders of the teachers and the department of education, which is not yet even focusing on upbringing but instead on educating. This is why the entire education system itself is falling apart.

I think that the internet, which is developing alongside the calling to become integral—alongside Nature's call to humanity—is the answer to the question, "How will we attain a global education and upbringing?" It can be done only through the internet. The internet is the least expensive platform, but it provides the best accessibility and can facilitate the creation of a new human being, one who is not restricted by any boundaries. Moreover, we won't just be forming a new human being, but a whole new world, which will be realized within him.

How is "the world" defined? The world is what we perceive. Indeed, if our sensations shift from egoistic to altruistic, the world will change as well, since we will perceive it differently. After all, the world is perceived by sensation, which means that it can appear to us in a completely different way.

This is the usual materialistic approach, the scientific one. We see that our perception or attitude toward reality completely changes the way we perceive reality. Hence, reality is relative.

Engels, Einstein, and all the newest theories, including psychological ones, agree on this. We are not saying anything new. We are simply inviting the world to see this global, integral upbringing as our new human level through which we actually enter Einstein's world of relativity, the world on the next level.

There are no distances in this world on the next level because distance is measured by our sensations, and our sensations will no longer repel one another, but will instead unite with each other. It's as if we overcome the distances between us. They become psychologically reduced to zero because we attain the principle, "Love your neighbor as yourself."

Thus, we achieve a state where time becomes restricted. Right now, time is between us due to our egoism. But if we are all inside a single sphere of desire, then practically speaking, time will not exist. Being in this sphere, we gradually accelerate time, contract space, and shift from the sensation of a physical world to the sensation of a virtual world.

This is Nature's call to unity. The call is not only for us to overcome the repulsion between us, but to raise us to a new level of perceiving life.

Many people are already starting to see the world this way. And we also see how youths aspire to reach this world and enter it.

CREATING A NEW, UNIFYING INTERNET

– Children are ready for the new reality, but parents are frightened by it. When we experimented with parents, it seemed like they were interested in the integral method, but as soon as they had a chance to try it out in practice, the habit of prohibitions was switched on. Also, parents are afraid of the internet and its possibilities, and try to control the information that children have access to, and indeed, many internet sites contain negative information. So what is the right way to allow a child to surf the internet?

– The internet is an absolutely free environment making it a double-edged sword: it can be a life giving elixir or a lethal poison.

Naturally, youths, with their hormonal surges, sensitivity to public opinion, intense emotional states, and inherent psychological instability, are subject to all sorts of risks. But I think that young people are attracted to communication. At our venues, they really are able to socialize with each other freely, and this socialization gives them a sense of "transcending" the negative influences, including those found on the internet.

There really is no choice in the matter: We must join the competition that is already on the internet, and I think this is a good thing. We will all learn from it and we will circumvent the obstacles in a way that will make us more appealing, while providing better answers to young people's questions.

We are in a war against powerful rivals whose goal is to sell our children anything that brings them profit. And usually, these things are bad for children. But this war is precisely the means that will enable us to find the right way to express ourselves in order to really reach the new generation.

These obstacles are first and foremost meant for us rather than for our children because it is how we will begin to understand our children. Through parents trying to break through to children by involvement in different sites—which are attractive because of their easy access, simplicity, and exposure— we will learn to understand the nature of the new society that we are trying to create. We adults are starting to understand nature's challenge. We are the previous generation while our children are the future generation. The transition from the past to the future happens precisely through the war over the new virtual space where humanity will truly unite.

Also, we are not at all against people being exposed to online sex. The only problem I see is sites that promote violence. Actually, even those are not such a big problem because they will dissipate. These violent sites display their greed, bile, and negativity, and people will begin to feel it and will not be attracted.

I think that we have to gradually explain our worldview as well as how it is activated by the law of Nature. We cannot change Nature's laws. We simply need to explain to people about the laws of development, the boundaries in which we exist and which we must carry out one way or another. And the earlier we do this, the better it is for everyone, since then we won't have to wait for the blows to force us to adhere to the conditions of Nature's laws.

THE REVELATION OF THE NEW WORLD IS IN COMMUNICATION

– What is so special about these internet venues of the new world? And how should they be fundamentally different from the ones that exist now?

– They have to give the new humanity, children, and youths the opportunity to connect with each other in a way that lets them conduct unceasing psychological analyses of themselves and the world. It is a connection that needs to show them how much the world depends on their psychological perception. Then their growing closeness, their exit from themselves and into others, will cause them to sense a new world. They will be enthralled by this mode of communication because they will have an enormous need for it.

The game of revealing this new world is truly fascinating. We need to create diverse psychological trainings and interesting games that demonstrate the proper method of upbringing, and how the world changes by the way we look at it. The world is relative, Nature is relative, and so are distance, space, and time. Everything unfolds in our sensations. This is what we have to show everyone.

Our current world is immobile, crusty, inflexible, and formal because we sense it through one quality—egoism—instead of two parallel qualities—egoism and altruism. When these two qualities constantly alternate in a person and intertwine in different ways, a powerful process occurs as that person begins to experience a new virtual adventure.

We need to create online venues where youths and adults of diverse mentalities can communicate freely even if they speak different languages (such as by using automatic translation). I understand that this may be difficult, but this is what we have to achieve—a point where humanity rises above language barriers, and in fact, above any differences! Then, through this type of communication, people will discover new states of being.

This process will become even more enthralling to everyone than any movie because we approach movies merely as spectators and only slightly associate ourselves with them. In the new type of communication, people will experience new states *within* them. They will go on internal adventures and experience such transformations that they couldn't possibly experience anywhere else.

Naturally, the various physical drives will remain, but they will only supplement this other experience. In principle, we consist entirely of a desire to enjoy and be satisfied. The satisfaction people will feel from the intense internal, psychological states will be the revelation of a new world! It will be so powerful that if it doesn't suppress our physical desires, it will at least turn people's attention—even young people—from hormones (although we are not against them) to the attainment of the new world and myself within it.

THE INTERNET ABOVE PHYSICAL CONTACT

– Is it advisable to have a gender or age division at the online venues where people will get together, or can the audience there be completely diverse, like in a natural situation where every person simply finds the closest and most interesting venue?

– Everything depends on the extent to which we will acclimate the internet, this virtual space. Today it is still in a rudimentary state. It will take great efforts to create new, suitable forms of communication there. There are no programs out there yet that can allow thousands of people to participate simultaneously in a forum, socialize, and see themselves in one virtual space as if they are in the same room. This is still very difficult to accomplish.

The internet has to raise us above the sensation of physical space. It has to create an illusion or the sensation of space, a feeling of being included in one another. We don't have such instruments yet, but I hope they will be developed.

We have to use what we have. We believe that Nature is error free, that it is leading us forward, giving us precisely the opportunities that we need in order to advance. We have to use these opportunities as an exercise to gradually prepare for the future states. Then these states will come and evoke the appearance of new technologies that suit them.

– Within this virtual communication, is there room for a person's individual talents and abilities?

– I think that differentiation will happen on its own accord. People will get together just as they do in a regular society, according to their characters, interests, and so on. I also think that there is no need to draw any distinctions between men and women. When we give people the chance to socialize, we should not place them in any sort of boundaries.

But of course, it's best if men would socialize more with men, and women more with women. On the other hand, it's very difficult for women to socialize in a purely female environment.

Men have to develop such connections that are not based on physical interests, but are on a higher level: the human level rather than the animate one. They have to have an opportunity to communicate, connect, befriend, and unite with one another apart from the female community.

We see that this division happens in every society: there is a male sector for men and a female sector for women. For example, even Hollywood, no matter how liberal it is, makes some movies that are intended primarily for men, and others for women.

You cannot do anything to change it. We are a part of Nature and we are naturally divided. This division between the sexes is the most vivid and the strictest. It divides everything from top to bottom, on all levels of Nature—still, vegetative, animate, and human.

Therefore, I think that our upbringing will also differentiate between people by gender. But they have to make this analysis on their own and find the best place for them to socialize, and decide the extent to which they must avoid the other sex in order to achieve unity, meaning unity of men with other men. Perhaps women can also unite in some way, but on a different level because men's unification is inherent in Nature, unlike women's.

THE ROLE OF THE INSTRUCTOR
IN THE UPBRINGING

– If children aged 9 to 12 find a venue and start socializing there, is it necessary for an instructor to participate in this process in order to guide them?

– The instructor is necessary because otherwise there won't be any upbringing taking place. Upbringing is when an older person who knows the youths' future states is present and helps them form that state. Also, the instructor must do it gradually, unnoticeably, such as by giving them hints.

The educator, or instructor, must be invisible. He is on their level. However, that is because he descended to this level from his own higher level in order to elevate the students to his own level. It's like an elevator that descends in order to elevate them. This is the role of the instructor.

Nonetheless, when he descends, he is on the same level as the children. The children don't feel that the instructor is special or a grownup. They see him as someone who's there to help them. He doesn't do anything special and doesn't give out any orders or try to rule over them in any other way. They should sense him as "Nothing more than we are."

His mastery lies in his ability to influence them gradually, from the inside, in a way that's imperceptible to the children. In this manner, he gathers them together and leads them to the decision to rise higher. He evokes this interest in them so their inner desires, questions, and various pressures gradually transform into a desire to unite, and thus rise to the next level. He has to give them hints about how to get together. On their own, they have no idea where their desires are leading them, but he inconspicuously monitors their direction through various hints and clues, while the children don't notice he is doing it. Then, suddenly they say, "Yes, this is exactly what we need," and they advance, without any doubt that they achieved this progress on their own.

This approach accords with the principle, "Raise a child according to his own way."

THE PARENTS' ROLE IN INTEGRAL UPBRINGING

– Parents want to monitor their children in some way and to participate in these processes. They try to intrude on these networks under assumed names in order to observe what their children are up to. Is this appropriate?

– To be your child's virtual friend?

– Yes! It's like opening your child's diary and reading it while he is out of the house. It's very important to understand what role a parent has to play and how he should participate in this process. Does he have a place there or not? How should parents acquire information?

- I don't see parents having any role in the virtual space. Parents have to understand that they have to be friends with their children and discuss everything with them, but not where the child does not want to see them. After all, he's not a child anymore. We are talking about teenagers, who are pretty much adults already.

The entire foundation of the future person is instilled at ages 6 to 9. After age 9 we only develop whatever was already instilled. In ages 9 to 13, it is already the period when one's personality forms.

Past the age of 13 there is nothing more that can be done to a person. It is very difficult to change anything in him! All of the data and values that were instilled in him acquire their final form.

This is a big problem. Parents think that this is still their little child! Even when the child turns 20, parents are still willing to run after him and give him orders, trying to protect him from everything. Parents must understand a very simple rule: They cannot intervene in the process of upbringing that we provide. Additionally, parents need to learn to apply the same method of upbringing with their child at home. This amounts to being simple, sincere, and friendly with the child, and showing him that you agree with his upbringing. This is how parents will earn the child's approval, so he won't consider them dinosaurs or worse, enemies. Parents have to show the child that they trust him, and in various ways they need to let him understand that they respect the child for taking the path to a new worThe self-respect that you awaken in a child with your attitude toward him is of utmost importance! It would be profoundly beneficial for parents to watch positively influenced television or internet programs together with their children, meaning programs that show the correct kind of communication models and relationships, including programs that depict all kinds of problems along with their solutions, like a movie for the whole family highlighting the topic of "fathers and sons," meaning gap between the generations.

– We found that the programs people were most interested in watching together were the ones where children talk about how they perceive their parents. This was very interesting! The children shown in the program were 12 years old, and for the first time in their lives the parents heard what they look like to their children.

There is a saying that goes, "Everybody knows how to cure people, how to run the government, and how to raise kids." What we found was that parents actually strive to perfect this method. They intervene and give their own advice.

How should the right kind of interaction with parents be set up? How can we give them room to be creative?

A METHOD FOR CHILDREN AND ADULTS

– I work with parents who are learning the integral approach and the system of unification. They find it interesting to participate in this process. They aren't just interested in waiting for the results from the children, but are convinced that they were born in a new world and deserve to feel it, that they deserve to exist in the integral, global humanity. Thus, both parents and children end up having a common interest, which is to transform themselves to suit the new matrix that Nature is presenting before them. That is why it is easy for us to find common ground between parents and children, since their aspirations are practically the same.

The fact that this is easy for children but difficult for parents cannot be changed because it is a transitional period. Transitional periods are never easy: There are all sorts of impulses, fluctuations, and deviations from the balanced state.

But this community lives in a unified movement, as if it were going through an extremely interesting adventure or hobby, and that goes for parents and children alike.

I think that we shouldn't take away from parents this opportunity to go through this positive change and reveal the new world. Their age is not an obstacle. If we involve them, then instead of being passive onlookers or even opponents, they will be active participants. This is our objective.

That is why we have to develop and disseminate the method of integral, global upbringing to all age groups.

– How does the method differ for adults and for children?

– It differs somewhat in the way it is implemented. The method for children involves studying with them for many hours at a time instead of regular school. The regular school program is reduced and replaced with an "educational hour," although it isn't really an hour, but many hours each day. Children take part in debates, forums, all types of socialization, and games.

Everything is aimed at showing a person that you can achieve positive results only when you are together with everyone. Everything that is not obtained together is negative.

This is a bit more difficult to show to adults. But then, you don't have to show adults everything using examples from life. Adults need logical explanations using examples from Nature. Children, on the other hand, are not impressed by logic. They need direct explanations and examples. So there is a difference in the method, but in principle, age doesn't matter.

– To realize the method among children, do they have to socialize and conduct discussions about what they saw and learned?

Adults mainly work internally, in their intention. Their communication with one another and the discernments they make are invisible. But should the parents also physically sit together in a circle like children and discuss things?

– We see that young people who fall in love are simply joined at the hip and go everywhere arm in arm. But afterwards their relationship settles into a calm phase when you simply exist together with the person you love and the two of you understand each other. You aspire to reduce the physical distance between you, but you no longer have the need to touch each other or to talk about your feelings.

In a sense, you shift to a "virtual" phase in your communication. You already understand and feel each other at a distance. You feel the solidarity which you have created in your relationship, so a calmer phase naturally sets in.

It is not that you stopped loving each other or that you don't want to feel each other physically. It is a connection that has emerged between you, which no longer requires constant physical complementing, expression, and proof. And the same thing happens here.

When you have a group of children that have just begun assimilating this method, it is necessary to influence them through songs, dancing, games, communication, forums, debates, and so on. But when you have a group of people who are already moving toward this unification, who are already forming it inside of them, and are daily studying the method of the integral, global upbringing, then they do not require external, physical, showy actions. They understand that everything is present in that internal formation, and their work is done without any words. It happens in their feelings, just as between people who are close and understand each other without any words.

That is how people gradually unite, as it is written, "One man with one heart." After all, a person does not talk with himself. Everything happens within him, automatically, even unconsciously. This is the kind of connection that has to emerge among people.

A DIFFERENTIAL, INTEGRAL APPROACH TO NATURE

For children, the process of learning about life is active and multifaceted. They have to learn how banks, hospitals, and depots work. They have to visit the zoo, fields where crops are grown, a planetarium, and so on.

Then, they should discuss how all these are interconnected. The concrete and fragmentary impressions of the world should eventually connect into a single, integral picture that will give them the impression of the world as one whole.

We are the ones who divide the worlds into parts, into still, vegetative, animate, and human levels. We also divide it into all kinds of sciences, but what sciences can there be in reality? It's all Nature! Nature is one. It is only we who divide it into disciplines such as biology, zoology, botany, and geography because of our limited perception, because we cannot grasp everything at once.

We have to show people that there is a differential approach, an integral one. We have to make these two approaches evident and let people understand that the world is now transitioning from differentiation and division into sectors and levels, to one that is integral and entirely interconnected.

Even though we receive fragmentary impressions about how factories and banks work, or planetariums, depots, and so on, afterwards, we have to unite everything into one, single humanity. That way, whenever children see any phenomenon in the world, they will be able to perceive it as part of the common whole, and will therefore never make the wrong decision.

All of today's crises are happening because we cannot approach the world integrally. This is why humanity keeps repeating the same mistakes. We cannot solve a single problem because we are not internally holistic. The only way to solve today's world's problems is by viewing the world as one whole. We have to talk to children about unity among people and how they can grow closer because this is the method of Nature. By doing this, we will awaken the single force of Nature and it will influence them. According to the law of equivalence of form, we will evoke the influence of Nature's upper force upon them, the force that unites and includes everything, including us.

THE CRITERION FOR SUCCESS IS MAN'S INTEGRITY IN THE ENVIRONMENT

- Every methodology has a criterion for evaluating its effectiveness.

In a regular modern school, a child's achievements are assessed by the amount of information he has learned, his diligence, his achievements in other fields, such as competitions, and so on.

What are the criteria for measuring the efficiency and success on the integral method, and how should these criteria be implemented?

- First, we do not give any grades or evaluations. We develop people the way they are. Every person has his or her own rate of development and you cannot compare people.

With today's children, the most important thing is not to suppress the new capabilities that are developing in them. That is why we should approach them without any grades or other measuring scales. The only criterion should be a person's integration with his integral environment.

But everything is relative in this regard as well. I see this in adults as well: Some learn very fast and advance quickly, but at some point they stop progressing. Others start out having a very hard time agreeing, and understanding what the study is all about. It takes them a very long time, often years, to hear this call to unite with others into one, single, whole desire, similar to the common force of Nature.

We have to understand that we were created this way, so we cannot give people grades. Each of us is utterly unique.

When a child or any person at all participates in this process to the best of his ability, this alone is praiseworthy and should be the person's only grade. Any kind of participation has to be valued because what's important is not one's success, but his participation!

– Suppose there were 10 meetings held with a group of children. One child participated in all 10 meetings and made efforts to create a common space, whereas another child showed up twice and was not very active. Can this be a criterion for assessing the effectiveness of the work?

– Definitely, because we are a product of society. If I am in this society for a long time, then of course I am influenced by it and become similar to it. 10 meetings with this society will influence me much more than if I accidentally show up there twice.

The number of meetings has to be fixed. And we have to view a person's progress accordingly.

However, it is easier and simple for some people to learn this because their egoism is not expressed as vividly. It is weaker. They advance faster even though they might have participated in communication with others less.

We have to understand that success can only be achieved through daily studies that last for many hours and include physical games, all sorts of discussions, reading, trips, excursions, and other ways to gain familiarity with the world.

THE SKILL OF ACTING IN UPBRINGING

Self-analysis is the most important thing. Therefore, it is very important to teach children the skill of acting. They have to be able to step out of themselves, put their "selves" aside, and play a different role. Say, I want to become another person. How do I imagine that person? How do I act him out? And how do I take my "self" and put it aside? This is the art of acting, and it is very important for a child. This enables him to impersonate and thereby understand others. Every child has to learn it, as well as psychology, and other techniques.

There has to be a very serious dialectic preparation, especially during the first several years of life, since the foundation of the future person starts forming at age 6 and is completed by age 9 or 10. After that it only develops.

– Can acting be used in the form of games already at age 6?

– Certainly! Children love playing this game because through it they get to know themselves. A child starts to understand: How do I look at the world and other people differently as I change? By doing that, children prepare themselves for the perception of a qualitatively new world.

– Based on your advice, we held a game called "a court case over egoism" where children exchanged roles. The children really enjoyed taking part in it, but interestingly, when we offered the adults to do the same, it frightened them and they refused.

– You see! This is why we have to work with children. They have to go through all the various situations in this court, experience different roles, and that way experience themselves from different sides: Now I'm playing the role of the accused, now I am the accuser, now I am his advocate, and now I just want to figure out what is happening to him, and so on. This way, they won't be afraid. But we, adults, do not understand this. We are closed off inside of ourselves. And yet, we have to raise our children to be free from themselves.

CREATING AN INTEGRAL ENVIRONMENT

- Hyperactivity Is the Adults' Problem, Not the Children's
- Shared Ownership of Resources
- The Need for the Appropriate Mass Media
- Making Sure Life Doesn't Teach Us with a Rod
- Similarity to Nature Is the Guarantee of Safety
- How to Occupy and Feed Seven Billion People
- What about Thieves and Other Criminals?
- Adults Are the Same Ill-Bred Children

I would like to talk to you about the concept of "boundary." When modern children get together, something very strange happens to them: It's as if they turn into uncontrollable animals. Adults constantly complain that children are unruly and don't yield to any upbringing. What is this that is happening and how should we relate to children's hyperactivity?

– Hyperactivity is the problem of our time. It has existed for several decades now, but we initially didn't recognize it. We first thought it was some kind of illness or disorder, but then we noticed that it is a phenomenon, and not long after, it turned into the norm. We have already discussed that the new generation is different: egoistic, nudged on from the inside by very powerful impulses that are of a completely new quality.

Therefore, we cannot approach them with the previous standards in order to decide whether their behavior crosses the line or not, because their "line" is new. In fact, everything with them is new. We call it hyperactivity, but for them it's normal.

HYPERACTIVITY IS THE ADULTS' PROBLEM, NOT THE CHILDREN'S

They cannot fit into our outdated boundaries, and this is not their fault but ours. Therefore, we must immediately revisit our behavioral standards and develop a different attitude toward children so we don't keep them "imprisoned" all the time. We are trying to impose our norms of behavior and our limitations on them. But they can no longer live that way.

In the past, people had no problem living their whole lives in the same village without ever leaving it. Today even the villagers are different: They feel they have to travel, to see many things and learn many things so that once they return to their village, they will still be connected to the world. People today are different!

Therefore, it is us that we have to curb, not the children.

– But this is very difficult because we have habits.

– Of course. And children are the easiest to break. But nothing will come out of it because that way we are breaking Nature.

Nature is showing us the new phase of its development. It's telling us, "Here he is, the human being of the future. He's not corrected, not finished, and not molded yet, but these are his true initial qualities, his desires, motions, and drives." This is a challenge that's being presented to us, and we have to respond to it.

– You call modern children "the people of the future." But many parents and teachers say that they are more like monkeys.

A woman I knew had a pet monkey at home and I had a first-hand experience that convinced me how unruly and dumb this animal is, destroying everything in its way. And now many people are ascribing precisely this behavioral model to their children.

– I am certain that if someone would take the right stewardship over this monkey, then it would start eating with a fork and knife, and would tie a napkin around its neck. And it would look wonderful sitting at the table.

If a person does not receive an upbringing, he will act as if he just came out of the jungle. Everything depends on the surrounding environment. Therefore, we have to create an environment for children, which corresponds to the demands of our era.

We cannot say, "We can't do anything with them because they are not like us." So what! Can we really treat our children that way, the most precious thing we have? It's astounding how egoistic we are.

A system of upbringing does not exist. The education system does exist because we want to get children off our backs, give them some kind of profession, and send them on their way. But upbringing is something we don't give them. We don't build people out of them. When we do something for children, we don't worry about their comfort, and we don't make it our objective to coordinate our actions with their nature.

Today there are enormous desires, urges, restlessness, and inattention being expressed in our children. Internally, they work at an enormous speed. What can we do to make things simple and easy for them, so they would feel good and free?

What difference does it make what kind of world we will build? It can be anything as long as the children are happy. That should be everyone's attitude toward their children. So why don't we feel that way? We, adults, are egoists, wishing to break them as it suits us, for our own convenience, and that's all there is to it.

SHARED OWNERSHIP OF RESOURCES

– In psychology, a "boundary" is determined as the place where my interests collide with the interests of the people around me. As it often happens, the desired resource is limited. In that case, two scenarios might unfold: Either I yield that resource to the other person, or I fight to possess the resource. Does the concept of the integral society, the human being of the future, lie in yielding or fighting?

– Neither. It's to affirm what is shared, and only what is shared. There is no "yours" or "mine." You and I must both own the resource together, and that doesn't mean each of us has his own half, but that the resource is shared. This is the goal of integral upbringing.

– When the Americans tried to civilize the Indians, they encountered a problem: The Indians did not have private property. They did not understand the meaning of "stealing" or "taking someone else's property" because everything was shared in their community.

– Now you are describing something similar. Does that mean there shouldn't be private property as such?

– That's right. The Indians did not have private property before the egoism emerged. Even now, for the most part, their egoism is at a very low developmental level. I am familiar with some of these people and I even had a chance to observe them in Canada.

But today we are at the highest peak of egoistic development. Our egoism is enormous, demanding constant satisfaction, regardless of everyone, and even in order to spite them. I enjoy being superior to others. The worse someone else feels, the better I feel.

At our current stage, we have to create a society in which I will feel that everything belongs to everyone, including myself, meaning that I belong to everyone and not to myself. There should be nothing in me that I could call my personal "self," but only "we" and "ours."

We, not the Indians, are the ones who have to achieve this today. This work requires enormous efforts, upbringing, and education, but when it happens, it will be a serious correction of man's nature. Through the corrected egoism, we will feel a completely different reality, a different world!

– Let me be more specific. Suppose there are five children and three chairs, and all five want to sit. How should the situation be handled?

– They should be brought up so that if there are not enough chairs, they wouldn't desire to sit on a chair, but would all prefer to sit on the floor, or at least they would all insist that someone else sits on the chair. We have to instill in them the understanding that if another person benefits, then I benefit too.

This is not easy, but children accept it naturally, especially at the age of 9 or 10. They grasp it much more naturally than 12 year old teenagers or young adults at 17 or 18. At that young age it's possible to create the prerequisites for solving the problems of "mine," "yours," and "ours."

THE NEED FOR THE APPROPRIATE MASS MEDIA.

– Social psychologies that study modern Western society say that this society is operated by the law of trade off: "You give something to me and I give something you." They say that even friendship is defined by this "You give me and I give you" concept, only in this case it is stretched out over time. This means that the modern person is entirely imbued in this idea of trade off, and what you are describing is a fundamentally different paradigm, a different worldview.

How can we, people who are pervaded by the law of trade off, by egoism, adopt a different paradigm and pass it on to our children?

– We have to create the appropriate mass media materials to influence people. The Communists in Russia dreamed of this. This is why they built the socialist system in the Soviet Union. But they did not achieve anything because they wanted to impose their worldview by force.

We do not impose our ideas on anyone. We are just showing people the state of the world and of Nature, the challenge Nature is presenting us with, and Nature's globality and integrality. It obligates us to be similar to it, while now we are the opposite of it.

We have no other choice but to explain that everything that is happening in the world is the result of our similarity or dissimilarity to the surrounding environment. We are the only ones who are not in harmony with the environment, and by that we cause all the problems and crises in Nature.

We have to create a system of upbringing that will constantly give us positive examples, every moment, through books, movies, internet, and television. Everything we see must unequivocally show us what is good for us and what is bad, in what regard are we similar to Nature and in what regard are we not, and in what way does this reciprocal connection operate.

Nature does not know mercy, and the sword is already raised over our heads, ready to strike. The law of gravity is unchanging.

You can talk to it and beg for mercy, but if you walk off the roof of a ten story house, you will fall from the 10th floor, whether you're a good person or a bad one.

In a society where everyone is connected as one single whole, everyone is under the influence of a single law, regardless of how you act. There is a condition called "mutual guarantee," by which everyone depends on everyone else, every person is responsible for everyone else, and no one has any obligation as a separate entity.

By constantly explaining where we are and what kind of trap we are caught in, by showing people that we have exhausted our options, we will create a system of upbringing that will change them. And whether we create it voluntarily or involuntarily depends on our sense of urgency.

For our survival, we must become similar to this system— integral and globally connected with one another and with Nature, just like all of Nature's other parts, because we are a part of Nature, we don't govern it.

- What you are now describing is evident only to researchers who study Nature in depth.

- But they can present us with all the necessary data. And when artistic people learn these laws, they will express them through various forms of mass media and by other means of mass communication. They will create plays and movies based on these laws, which could be shown alongside the current movies that depict a horrible end to civilization. This can help people understand precisely why everything is happening as it is, and how we can correct everything. This will help them see that Nature already has the forces of correction.

MAKING SURE LIFE DOESN'T TEACH US WITH A ROD

– You say that a child has to be raised in a way that lets him perceive the world holistically from early childhood.

– Yes, only this way. After all, we are in a global world. This is already clear to many people. After all, we teach children to be adapted to the world.

– Is it a good idea to place a globe in front of a 3 year old child and spin it around?

– Certainly, even before the age of 3. Even if he still doesn't understand what a globe is, let him play with this ball. The child will retain an impression of it.

You might not be aware of it, but there are pictures in your subconscious, recollections from a very early age, practically from age 0 and up to one year old. They can be evoked: There you are lying down, you are being diapered, fed, and washed. You don't see yourself or the world yet, but something is already there. In every baby, there is an adult looking out from the inside, while the body is still small. We don't notice it because we pay attention only to the body.

The images and ideas that a child grasps before the age of 9 or 10 are the foundation of his development. After that he only forms and realizes them, but it's no longer possible to change anything.

If we don't build the right foundations in a child, if we don't give him the right upbringing during these years, it will be impossible to raise him afterwards. He will already have other ideas, other examples of behavior and relationships. Therefore, it has to be done literally from age 0, or at least starting with age 3.

– When teachers and parents interact with children, they come up against the problem that it is difficult to work with the child because he is very unstable. One moment he's running around, and the next moment he's yelling, falling on the floor, and wallowing there. Or, he can leave the room because that's what he felt like doing all of a sudden. Should we limit him or somehow use this dynamic?

- You shouldn't do anything to him. You have to create a deliberately integral environment around him. That's all. This means that in that environment he depends on everyone and everyone depends on him. He has to understand this without explanations, but if necessary, you can explain it to him by showing him the world.

Who are you? You are a guide to the world in which he found himself. This means that you have to show him this world and demonstrate how it works. Show him how you treat others, how others treat you, how you share with others and do something for them. He has to see all of this.

And gradually, based on these extremely subtle interconnections, show him that if he doesn't participate in everything together with everyone and does not take others into consideration, if he does not desire to be integrally connected with them, then others won't treat him the way he wants either. And this is the reason for his suffering.

Then a child will start to understand this system from the inside, to study it from life. After all, life is teaching us with a rod, with little disappointments: This is how you were treated, this is what your mom or babysitter did, or the children around you. That is, he has to receive punishment, but also the appropriate reward for having the right attitude to the integral environment.

- Suppose that during some common activity, a child came up to the teacher and kicked him. This actually happens.

- If you take an unprepared child from the street and bring him into this kind of system, then of course he will experience horrible states because he will not understand anything.

We are talking about children who started receiving the right upbringing from birth. We have to make our lives easier in some way. We cannot break children who have already formed egoistically, so we have to start with children who have been prepared.

After that, it is possible to gradually begin to accept uncorrected children into this environment, meaning those who grew up in the uncorrected environment. Once we have a strong environment, we can introduce others into it and correct them. That's because correction happens only under the influence of others' example.

SIMILARITY TO NATURE
IS THE GUARANTEE OF SAFETY

– Parents worry that a child growing up in this kind of society may become excessively dependent on the opinion of others and will lose his independence.

– I think that's nonsense. The greatest force that provides everything in the world is the force of Nature. If I am similar to it, then I have nothing to fear. I won't be weak, constantly protecting myself, living in fear, and expecting a blow. This kind of life really is worse than death. On the contrary, I will be strong, independent, sensible, calm, and balanced.

Besides, I cannot imagine a normal parent telling his child, "Be strong and arm yourself. Someone five feet away from you just spit; go kill him. Someone behind you cursed; turn around and shoot him." We guide children to be gentle to the people around them because this is the safest for our children. We say, "Don't talk back," "Go some place else," "Don't be around these people," "Treat others properly and kindly." This creates a favorable environment around a child and reduces the probability that someone will hurt him.

Parents have always instructed children to be gentle, kind, move away from harmful or evil things, and closer to good things. It is the same in every society, especially in a global and integral society, which is where we are.

Even if such a person is an athlete and physically strong, he won't use that force negatively. He will have developed his body because he wants to feel confident, but without getting into an aggressive mindset from the start.

– Now that we have begun to implement this method, the question of studios or workrooms arose, meaning places where a child can realize his unique abilities, such as singing, playing musical instruments, learning math and sciences, and so on.

Also, at some age, children start needing to learn some kind of marshal art. Is there any point in creating a class like that?

– We think that all games have to be played in teams. If the whole team wins, then I feel like the winner together with others, but I should never feel like I stand out. Games have to be part of upbringing. But if I set one person against another, this goes against Nature's demand.

Maybe this skill can come in handy in certain circumstances. But in truth, I don't see how people who know combat skills can be successful, how they will defend themselves this way, and how this will enable them to save their own lives and the lives of others.

I think that all of this is just the advertising done by the owners of these clubs. Nature does not have any apparent evidence that it is necessary to be physically strong or to have the upper hand over others. Not only do individual people differ from one another, but so do nations: Some are more physically enduring and strong, and others are weaker. But this does not affect anything.

Only one's similarity to Nature brings every person and every nation as a whole to a comfortable state.

HOW TO OCCUPY AND FEED SEVEN BILLION PEOPLE

– In different societies, people perceive the notion of "mine" differently. Some consider only their apartment to be their own and don't care what is happening on the bus or in the subway, so they throw their garbage on the floor there. But another person considers an entire city his own. Does the integral person you describe consider the whole world his own?

– Yes, but he gets there gradually. We cannot demand everything from people all at once. We shouldn't focus on individuals but on the social environment instead, because this is what raises him. We have to create such surroundings around a person that bring him up the right way.

Today an enormous amount of people are unemployed throughout the world. On the other hand, a slew of superfluous products are being produced. If we free up the people who produce the superfluous products, we will discover that only half a billion out of the 6.5 billion people in the world *need* to work, while the rest have nothing to do. So how will they feed themselves?

People will be paid for creating the right social environment. There must be global, regional, municipal, and neighborhood organizations whose only purpose and activity is to promote the concept of the integral way of life.

If this is your job, then you are an educator for everyone else. You have to make movies, ads, pictures, and books about this, and you have to talk about it. Your job is to walk around the streets and smile at everyone you see. That's right! There will be work for everyone, while half a billion workers will feed the others without producing anything excessive or polluting the earth.

This approach gives people the right intention. They start treating others kindly because that is their obligation, but meanwhile, others perceive this as the norm of the new behavior.

It doesn't matter that they receive money for acting that way. What's important is that they turn habit into a second nature, evoking Nature's favorable influence on them because they become similar to it.

Only now are we beginning to study the influence of our thoughts and desires on Nature. It's striking how even animals and plants perceive goodness and start treating us differently. And people are even more sensitive than flowers and animals.

By becoming similar to Nature, we will evoke an enormous positive influence on the world and it will truly change. To accomplish this, we need to create a good system of upbringing, involving billions of unemployed people in it who will do precisely this work.

It will require about half of humanity to raise the young generation. This won't require teachers of various disciplines, but educators—people who will give youths examples of the right behavior in a global society. There has to be as many educators as there are people being raised.

Then we will find ourselves in that integral mechanism into which Nature is forcing us. Suddenly, like a clutch in a car, we will start connecting like cogwheels, "click," and I am connected, unable to move anywhere alone. Now what should I do?

This mechanism should also contain proper cogwheels that say, "You do not have to spin together with everyone. Annul yourself and you will see that everyone is spinning just the way you want them to." When you do this, then you acquire freedom.

– When you describe this picture, it makes me remember my childhood. We also had times when we acted together. There was a wonderful atmosphere when we built snow castles together, for example. But then bullies would come, destroy everything we built, and beat us up.

Do you think that if we build this system correctly then there won't be any bullies?

– Imagine that you are hiring 3 billion people to work and you are starting to train them. They don't do anything yet besides being students at your university. Everyone is sitting in front of screens, studying via this worldwide virtual channel. Each person is learning in his own language about the world they live in, and they are getting paid for it. They write papers and reports, and study just as in school, from age 20 through old age. The hungry and homeless are given all the necessities, and the work for which they are paid is to study and do homework.

Everyone has to go through this kind of schooling and get a diploma that will enable them to live comfortably. After six months, you appoint them as educators in this system for half a day, while continuing to study during the second half of the workday. Gradually, they enter this system on their own and begin to behave the way they are taught among them and with others.

By providing the necessary work for everyone, you create a normal atmosphere. Nature becomes balanced and stops punishing you with earthquakes, tsunamis, and hurricanes. We evoke these problems ourselves because the human mind, desires, and drives influence Nature more than anything.

WHAT ABOUT THIEVES AND OTHER CRIMINALS?

– Like many uncorrected people, I still have many questions, worries, and fears: What will happen to criminals, thieves, and other people who might use this delicate reality, built on an ultra-sensitive balance? What if they come and steal everything, and take over the whole system?

- Do you understand that half of the earth's population is involved in this system? Who can go against it? Where are the thieves, activists, and criminals? They will be simply squashed by the masses and won't be able to poke their noses out. Besides, they, too, will be offered a decent living, a salary equal to everyone else. I don't think such difficulties will emerge.

There will be many problems, but they are all solvable because there is no other way for us to go. Nature is forcing us to solve them. If we don't do what Nature dictates and don't balance ourselves with it, it will be our end. You can intellectualize and philosophize as much as you want, but there is a law of Nature operating here.

Today, half of humanity is hungry and the other half doesn't know what to do with all the extras that it has. Correcting this imbalance will establish a normal human society.

Most importantly, human society must be similar to Nature, internally balanced, kind, and good. Then we will no longer have to fear being annihilated.

- I understand that you don't like the word "punishment," but shouldn't there be some sort of firm hand present, like a rod that if spared will spoil the child? From what you say, it seems like there is no place for this at all.

- No, of course there's a place for it.

- In what form, how?

- In the form of very powerful social reproach. But it has to be weighed so it won't kill "the human" in the person, so it won't trample on his dignity. A person has to be influenced by respect, by public approval; he can't be influenced in any other way.

The last, most notorious criminal is also proud, "I am a thief in my own right. Look at who I am; look at my jail! Respect me!"

There is no means more powerful on negative elements in society than to give them opportunities to elevate themselves, or vice versa, to place them in an environment that looks down on them.

They have an exaggerated attitude to their own "I," which is easy to play on. They are really little children who can be manipulated in any which way by giving them the opportunity to shine, or to the contrary, by slightly upbraiding them, showing that certain actions will lower him in the eyes of others.

– I am an adult who is surrounded by children. Suddenly one of the children does something that makes me upset. Can I show the child that it upsets me?

– That won't be upbringing. A child is raised by the surrounding environment that is equal to him. Therefore, your dissatisfaction has to be expressed through his peers. To him they are a respected environment and their opinion is important, whereas an adult is somewhere up above. His emotions are perceived by a child like thunder from the sky. You "thunder" at the whole world, but you are not next to me, you are not mine. So don't step forward against the child and turn him into an opponent. That will just make his egoism bigger. Instead, just place him in a neutral position and show him the right way to act using an example of someone else.

The way to have an influence on children is by having them discuss, judge, defend, and research themselves while watching videos of their behavior. Show children fragments of their behavior and let them discuss their actions. That's how a child will start to understand that if he were in that situation again, he would not act the same way.

The most important thing in our upbringing is teaching children through examples. This enables them to hold debates and analyze others' behavior, and then relate this experience to themselves.

ADULTS ARE THE SAME ILL-BRED CHILDREN

– The picture of the future school where children interact this way is very attractive for many people who are familiar with it. Can the same examples be used for adults?

– Adults are the same ill-bred children; they are just unaware of it. You see what they do on TV and what kind of conversations they have: They talk about how to get married, how to lose weight, or how to cook some dish. People are drawn to socializing.

Socializing is the most important thing for people, especially the kind of socializing that allows you to snoop into real life. Therefore, the kinds of discussions we have with our children at our education center are the most useful kind for society. These discussions just have to be formed properly and eloquently, so they are attractive and dynamic. If we form programs in this way, they will be the most in-demand TV programs; I am certain of that.

People who did not receive the integral upbringing in childhood don't know how it is possible to come out of yourself and place yourself on the side while placing another person inside of you, how to place yourself in someone else's shoes or take another's qualities into yourself. If people were not taught these techniques, then they don't know how to interact with each other correctly, so of course they are miserable. They wander about as if they're in the dark, bumping into each other, quarreling, and getting ofChildren have to be taught how to "dress" in each other, how to understand other people, how to accuse someone else, defend him, help him, and harm him, so everything is researched by every child through examples in life, both in groups and in TV programs.

We have to start preparing to bring the entire population of the world into the new educational system. Without it we won't survive. It doesn't matter how old a student is, if he's an adult or a child. Children study in this system throughout an entire day, and we have to do the same thing for adults.

The half billion people who will service all the others will also study in this system: They will study for half a day and will carry out the necessary jobs during the second half. We have to do this because otherwise humanity won't survive.

We are entering a system in which we are all cogwheels. Under the influence of the clutch pedal—Nature—we are beginning to make contact with one another. Soon we will start spinning together. I already feel how I am being locked together with others, but when I express even a little bit of my independence, I discover problems.

The reason for all the crises is that we are not spinning together. As a result, the system starts jamming and we stop spinning. This is a picture of collapse, worldwide crisis in all realms of life.

What will we be left with? How will we service one another? Nature will start excluding us. It has already practically excluded Japan, the Near East countries, and Russia from the entire world production. Look at what is happening to America, at what a downward spiral it is on. And what will happen to other countries? Will we get to a point where the only thing remaining in the world will be terrorism as the progressive form of activity? Everything is declining, and only terrorism is rising and flourishing. What have we come to?

I think we will overcome our resistance and understand that only worldwide education and upbringing, where every person is obligated to study, will lead us to harmony and peace.

GETTING TO KNOW YOURSELF

- Recognizing Yourself
- Find Your Own Answers to Your Questions
- Don't "Smudge" Yourself through Life
- The Group Must Be Homogenous
- Within the School Walls or Out in the Open?
- Reward Is the Energy Generator
- The Truth about Life Is Not that Scary
- Learning to Live from Life Itself
- Teacher's Pet

I am interested in the psychological aspects of the method of integral upbringing. Psychology has been an applied science for the past 100 years or so. Throughout this time researchers have developed various methods and tests, projective tests, and trainings. Can the experience acquired by materialistic psychology be used in the program of integral upbringing of children?

– It's interesting that humanity has existed for hundreds of thousands of years, and psychology, the science about man and about what he is, has existed for only a century. Can you imagine how long it took us to even start thinking about who we are? We evolved completely automatically, under the pressure of internal forces, desires, and thoughts, without ever stopping to think, "Why? What for? Who are we? Why were we formed this way? What causes our thoughts, feelings, desires, and aspirations?"

There is a striking, incomprehensible proportion between the hundreds of thousands of years of our development, and the one hundred years of the desire to understand who we are.

Everything flowed so calmly for such a long time. Even the greatest minds were not very interested in this problem, and that is one more piece of evidence that we have only recently begun to recognize ourselves as distinct entities in the world. We are distinct, and the world is distinct, but what is the connection between us and the world?

– But now people's interest in the questions, "What is the 'I'?" "How do we interact?" "How can we improve our interactions?" is rising exponentially.

– And the theories about it change at an astounding rate! I imagine the modern psychologist as being a very unstable person.

– This is really so. However, some very interesting tests have been developed. Can children go through those tests in order to get to know themselves better, to understand how they are built and what qualities they have? Or should we not let them go through these tests?

– We have to raise the next generation in a way that will give it the right attitude to life and to itself, so that people can test themselves. It is our obligation, the duty of parents and educators, and in fact, of anyone who cares about children. After all, they are our future! In 15 to 20 years, this generation will be in charge and we will disappear into history. We have to film them, show them films about themselves, and analyze their behavior from various angles, from the perspective of encouragement, defense, approval, and criticism.

RECOGNIZING YOURSELF

We have to enable every person to see himself from absolutely every angle, to come out of himself, to evaluate himself objectively and agree with the fact that he can be in completely different guises. One has to learn to accept all people: Yesterday he was that way and today he is different. It's very important to internalize that the perception of the world depends on me, on my mood, on the level of my development, and that it could change entirely. Whatever I am permitted, others are permitted, too. But all of this requires very serious study.

Incidentally, children's perception is much more pliant than that of adults. We should simply inculcate within them a soft, "flowing" point of view of things, and they will use it correctly. Everything depends on their views of themselves, the world, and others that we can instill within them.

– Getting back to the question of tests, when we deal with results of tests, there is a problem of confidentiality. We said that in a small group of children, nothing should be concealed. So should test results be put on the table for open discussion?

– I don't think the question should be put that way at all. If we approach the problem integrally, then all the children in all the schools in the world spend several hours a day working on self-analysis, self-discussion, and self-attainment. "Self-attainment" is the best word because through yourself you perceive the world, discern who you are, and accordingly, how you see the world. In such a state there is no question of whether you should disclose these tests or not.

These are not tests, but only a discussion. They can be displayed completely freely anywhere, even on TV. What is there to conceal? This is how children act and this is how they think.

I think that today the programs adults like most are programs about themselves. They're called "reality shows." People sit in a studio and talk about all sorts of problems.

I don't think the analysis should be turned into something that's concealed. Why do that? What could be secret about it? In fact, what could be secret about a person in general!? Don't psychologists understand this?

A person has animalistic as well as social urges inside of him, and they shouldn't be concealed. On the contrary, they should be revealed and discussed. A person has to understand how productive these urges can be for him in relation to others and to himself, so he can evaluate himself correctly and be comfortable with himself.

Instead of concealing things, everything should be exposed for everyone to learn from. It's not a discussion about someone, but a general learning process so every person will turn into his own therapist, and then he won't have to see therapists later on.

– Which don't help anyone at all, by the way...

We are talking about the notion of group processes. But what if something suddenly happens to someone and the educator takes a child aside and starts individually figuring out what happened to him, and having a "heart to heart" conversation with him? Is this also something that doesn't belong in this system?

– Absolutely not! Everything has to be brought out of the realm of the child's individuality, or even be specific to the group. Everything should be treated as a phenomenon. Perhaps it shouldn't even be treated or addressed on the same day. However, the approach should depend on the group's level of preparation and on its level of perception, on the children's ability to perceive themselves in different ways and to understand that "all that is happening reflects who we are."

– There are two conceptual approaches: One approach is to act according to a scenario that was planned ahead of time, and the other is to act according to how the process unfolds. For example, the second approach is when something has just happened to a child and we discuss precisely what is relevant right now. Is it better to act this way or to go according to a scenario that was planned ahead of time?

Incidentally, pedagogy and psychology radically disagree on this. Psychology prefers the process, "If a person is going through this right now, then this is what we'll talk about." And pedagogues say, "No, everything is planned out. Let's study according to plan." What's the right way to arrange this process?

- I think that all situations should be filmed. Today there are cameras everywhere—in cities, in the streets, and in parks. We, too, should put them everywhere, at all the venues where children go, including schools and school playgrounds.

We have to try to sort out their relationships and behaviors, or let the children suggest a topic for discussion, such as, "I have a certain relationship with one person or another. I think this way and others think differently, they don't agree with me. Let's talk about it."

Each child should be asked to play opposite roles, to be in the right, left, and neutral role, "I am right" and then "I am wrong," meaning I "move" into another person and from there I observe myself and discuss or condemn him. Or I am a "neutral person," like a jury in court.

I think these discussions are the most important factor for a person's formation because they let him develop on the inside. They expand his understanding of himself. He learns that "I can be one way, and the world can be completely different depending on how I look at it, and other people are like that too." Everything becomes very multi-faceted, flowing, and relative. And that's how the world really is.

– Can we talk about this more specifically? For example, suppose we have a meeting where we planned to discuss some phenomenon in the world, but one of the children comes to the meeting with a black eye. What do we do? Do we continue the discussion as planned, say about butterflies, or do we relate to his bruise and talk about it?

– Should we immediately discuss what happened together with him? But we don't know whether he will be able to come out of his state and reason about it. Maybe it should be handled differently: We don't pay any attention to his bruise, and have a "so what" attitude toward it. Meaning, we accept him the way he is, "This is your business. Sort it out yourself. To us you are a regular person. Right now we're talking about butterflies. Can you talk normally after you had a fight, or are you completely wound up and agitated?"

In this way we will still pay attention to what is happening to him, but from the opposite side. Here everything depends on the educator; I cannot give you any formulas. But this has to be viewed from the point of view of pedagogy: To what extent can this influence one's analysis of oneself and the world? Maybe he should talk to us about butterflies now, after this fight he had on the street? Or perhaps it's to the contrary: to stir him away from his thoughts, which distracted the group and prevented him from joining it, we should give him some special task or role and make him a hero, thus manipulating him into a completely different state. Or, using his example, we can show how one incident has distracted all of us from our topic. Meaning, he has practically disrupted all of our plans. An educator should see all of this and decide.

FIND YOUR OWN ANSWERS TO YOUR QUESTIONS

– Psychology attributes great importance to two notions called "mixed messages" and "direct messages." A classic example of a mixed message is to tell a joke, while a direct message is to answer a child's question seriously and directly. What is the more correct way to interact with children: To answer their questions directly, or is there room for jokes and games?

– The best thing is for someone to ask a question and then to find the answer by himself. When he asks you a question, it might very well not be a question at all, that he is just asking it to distract you or to distract himself, or that he wasn't the one who came up with it but just overheard it somewhere.

A question is a need to receive a certain informational or sensual fulfillment. Does this necessity exist in him? Did it ripen in him or not?

Therefore, the best approach is to bring a child—or any person, for that matter—to a state where he finds his own answer to the question. This means that he really ripened on the inside for receiving the answer, for fully realizing it, for absorbing it, and afterwards, for applying the conclusion he reached on his own.

Therefore, I would never give anyone answers to anything. It is precisely through all sorts of debates, court cases, discussions, conversations, and forums that children hold with each other, aided by educators, as well as trips to different places, followed by discussions of what they saw, why and how they saw everything differently that children learn how to find their own answers. They also hear questions that others ask, and that induces questions within them. They develop those questions, understand them, and find answers to them. This approach expands a child's perception and creates an expansive world within him, through which he sees the external world correctly, in a multi-faceted manner.

– So in essence, a child goes through the process of self-attainment and self-analysis?

– Yes, by discussing things with others. A person can never achieve anything alone, through personal attainment. He has to integrate with others. It is precisely the diverse and conflicting views that he accumulates that develop his perceptual abilities.

DON'T "SMUDGE" YOURSELF THROUGH LIFE

– Another important aspect in psychology is the "experience cycle," the preparation and choice of how to act, the act itself, and the completion and integration of the experience that resulted.

How important is it to ensure that projects started by the children achieve completion? If the children started doing something, should we encourage them to bring the process to completion?

– Bringing things to completion is a must! And in the process, everything must be described, filmed, completed, and documented. Clear conclusions must be drawn from it, which should be very concise so everyone can understand them even when they are expressed in a few words.

– That way we train a child to demand to make every situation in life concrete and real. Later, this will be of great help to them in making sure they don't "smudge" themselves through life, but always use their experiences to the maximum and learn from them.

The children went on an excursion, and then had a discussion. Maybe they created some kind of new boundaries or rules of behavior for themselves. All of this has to be documented, and the discussions should be minimal. The most important thing is the conclusion. It makes a person practical, preparing him for any form of activity.

- A person's professional identity is an extremely important part of his general identity. Should a child find his professional identity in this group as well?

Meaning, the children sit and decide, "You, Johnny, will be better off being a plumber. And you will turn out to be a good scientist..." Should a child solve these questions in a group setting as well?

- If we don't develop a child in connection with others, then we will never discern what his inclinations are. That's because by himself, a person is a small animal. His inclinations are expressed precisely in his connections with society, with the surrounding environment.

Any form of our activity is aimed at the connection between us. Even if I study butterflies, it means that society somehow "delegates" me to that activity. I have to understand my significance, the fact that someone needs this.

First we have to spend several years studying with children from ages 5 or 6 to ages 10 or 11. This includes making them included in one another as well as visiting various sites—industrial, scientific, medical, and social locations, which will gradually let them understand the various areas of people's activities.

Every time these trips are discussed, all the information must be documented. Every child will write a short report, through which we will begin to see the child's approach and discern his interests. For example, he may like to connect and bend tubes, so maybe he really will turn into a plumber. Or maybe he's interested in how people are cured. Or he likes collecting plants or butterflies, and so on.

Depending on how he describes what happens—with a physical or mathematical inclination, or in a sensitive manner—we will be able to see his inclination, either toward humanities or toward concrete matters. Gradually everything will be made clear, and the constant discussions will let the most important thing surface: Me in relation to others. This is a person's profession.

After all, a profession means that "I service other people and society in some way." This defines my place in society, my salary in it, and my position. I can only find that place after taking in many impressions, discussions, and sensations of everything that surrounds me.

Just asking a little child, "Who do you want to be?" Is an incorrect approach. But between the ages of 4-5 and 11-12 (no later than that) we can already see a person's inclination with absolute clarity.

13 is the age to become a university student. I think that as part of our upbringing, from around age 13 a child should start studying in a university program. By 17 or 18 he should graduate from university, meaning receive what is today considered higher education. After that he really will be professionally fit for a specific type of activity.

A child has to be taught to self-develop, to observe himself and others, and how to communicate with others. But the most important thing is to teach him to understand the world he lives in. A person has to understand his essence and his goal in life.

The integral, global education, or better put—upbringing—develops a person so much that it won't be difficult for him to study any science. That's because first, people talk to him about the world as a whole, about the general history and the general global system. And second, they explain that physics, biology, and chemistry are fragments of a huge global system: Nature.

We will not be able to grasp it and absorb it at once, but we can absorb fragments. If you cut a little piece of a huge cake, then you can eat that piece. But you can't swallow the whole cake all at once. This is what the separate sciences are, such as when we study biology, which examines living cells, tissues, and so on.

A child relates to the study as a particular field that is not so frightening. He looks at everything from the outside. And even if he delves deeper and deeper, he does not sink into it or becomes confused between "Where is all of this happening and where am I?" He looks at everything objectively. He can absorb all the knowledge instead of drowning in it, and this is very important for children!

I often see how children are afraid of the enormous amount of knowledge thrown at them. Every day they are presented with a multitude of formulas, going from one lesson to the next. Physics is followed by math, then biology, and then history. A child simply shuts himself down, and in the end does not absorb anything. He finishes school formally and retains impressions of it, but most of those impressions are from things that happened during breaks rather than in the classroom.

What's important is precisely this integral, global approach that reveals the world to a person. Children have to discuss the lessons themselves as well as the way they are held, in addition to all of their trips, and their impressions of these things. From a young age, children should have the opportunity to participate in the world the right way: go out to various events at least twice a week, get to know how things work: an airport, a hospital, a depot, nursing and retirement homes, factories, and so on. Then the children will feel that they are preparing themselves for the real woChildren study in school and at the same time learn about the outside world. They are shown the kind of knowledge that is necessary for living in it. That is how one's preferences for a profession become clear, as well as one's attitude to the world.

In a regular school they are simply forced to study. But in this case they already understand why they need this knowledge.

And even if I don't really need to know how yogurt is made, I still know that I need yogurt, and that means I'll look at how it's produced. After all, someone will make it, while in the meantime I will work with motors, for example. This means a lot! I don't have to be a doctor, but I know why and how a hospital works.

The most important thing is to show children that we are included in one another and that all of our professions exist for the sake of creating the correct social interaction. Then they will start having a very calm attitude to their studies. Children won't be bothered or scared by the prospect of starting university at age 13, even considering that they are regular children and not exceptional in any way. They have simply expanded their boundaries, their attitude toward the world, so the world doesn't scare them. The most important thing is to overcome fear.

THE GROUP MUST BE HOMOGENOUS

– Currently, the process of upbringing and education is structured sequentially, so if a child falls out of the process at some stage due to an illness or some other circumstance, it is often very difficult or even impossible for him to reenter it.

Is the method we are talking about open? Meaning, can a child start participating in it at any given moment? Or should we nevertheless make sure that the level of the children's preparation is approximately the same?

– We definitely have to take a child's level of preparation into consideration! If a child got sick or something happened to him that forces him to be absent for a period of time, then we have to make the whole group, the whole class participate in that.

It's better not to call it a class because this creates a negative association with a social class, with some kind of separation. A group is something friendlier, a setting where everyone are friends and equal. Whenever any person lags behind, the whole group should support their friend.

The group should be more or less homogenous. And even if someone joins it after the group has been formed, it should only be done when there are no other options, and very carefully. It will be necessary to give that child some time to prepare, go through a "crash course" so he can tune into the general flow and method, and will understand the group's outlook on life, and that is not easy to do.

But we have had cases of children from the outside joining the group successfully. They go through a conflict, but they overcome it and become part of the group.

Still, I think that this period traumatizes both him and the group. And it's clear how difficult this is for everyone and for him. It leaves a scar that remains there no matter what.

We understand that life is life and we are in a transitional period from the egoistic world to the integral world, but we have to try to protect the groups we are creating and lead them carefully, so they are open to all, yet open precisely because they know and understand each other. But it's very difficult for them to just allow someone to join them.

WITHIN THE SCHOOL WALLS OR OUT IN THE OPEN?

When we describe this method, we underline that the best result is achieved when a child goes through all the phases of development, starting from the right kind of conception, through the prenatal period, followed by the period of nursing, and so on.

- But that's how Nature is arranged as well. Do you see how it starts out? We evolve from a drop of semen, and we have to take this into consideration in our subsequent development as well.

Look at early, primitive societies: A child grew and was naturally included in the process of life. Once he reached a certain age, he could mingle with the adults. As he grew, he could increasingly participate in their activities. That is how he naturally joined the process together with his peers.

But what happens with us is that by putting a child in school, we cut him off from the life around him, creating artificial, impertinent conditions. And in addition, we prolong the period of school study. Starting with age 6, we sit them down behind a desk for the next 12 years. When I was a child there were only 10 grades. And as soon as children finish school, they have to go to college. And after college there are additional studies. The end result is that a person doesn't take part in the broader social life, and only by age 25, sometimes even 30, does he join the common system.

We have to arrange things so the study is completely integrated with his participation in the life of the society. And that shouldn't happen when he has already become an adult (considering that by age 16 or 17 he is already an adult), or when he finishes school and is thrown out to real life, not knowing what it is. This causes him to be under great stress.

Until now he was forgiven for everything, everything he did was praiseworthy, and everyone did everything for him: here's a ready to eat lunch, clean laundry, and some pocket money. He received full service for many years, and suddenly he is told, "Go and do everything for yourself, and make your own living." But no one prepared him for that. He was stuffed with some kind of unnecessary knowledge (if even that, because maybe he just sat in class all these years without even listening).

All this time should be used for raising a person in society! But this is not being done. A person is raised artificially within four walls of some learning institution, and after that at different clubs and parties, which are artificial as well. This is not enough. We have to let him take part in real work. We have to let him feel like an adult long before he actually becomes an adult and enters adult life.

I would open up a bank account for children after a certain age and would hire them to do community service jobs for which they would receive a certain salary. That is, they should start "playing" life in a way that's close to reality. The benefit of this will be tremendous, both for them and for society. They will understand their parents better and will develop a sense of responsibility. This is how we will gain a human being.

– In Soviet Russia there was an educator named Makarenko who worked with street children and juvenile delinquents. He is notable for demonstrating that a child's correction takes place under the influence of a constructive, creative activity. Under his management the children assembled FED cameras, which was the only thing that gave some kind of results.

Within your program of upbringing, can groups of boys or girls take part in some project, create certain values, and earn money by doing it?

– The projects they work on have to be necessary. We let them film things, then edit the video and audio materials, as well as texts about education and upbringing.

On the one hand, this turns them into specialists: They learn to work with computers, video, audio, and texts. They work with the materials and publish the results of their work on the internet. And in the process of working on creating these materials, they acquire specific skills that will help them with their professional orientation later on. In addition, they become creative.

On the other hand, this helps them understand themselves. That's because the children are working on their own material and experience it on themselves.

For example, they visited a factory, then a planetarium, and then a hospital. They have to film all of it, discuss it, and edit it. So they have a lot to keep them busy. We don't have time to give them some kind of "irrelevant" jobs. This is similar to what we had in school when I was a child. We had a class called "handcrafts," and I liked this class very much. This type of work develops a person.

Besides, we hold large unity events where children work together with adults. This lifts them up tremendously and lets them feel that being together with everyone is important. That is how they work, and that is how life is arranged.

REWARD IS THE ENERGY GENERATOR

– Suppose a group of children carried out some kind of project and completed it. Should we reward them in some way? Can an adult praise a child?

– Of course he can! We make it a point to do that whenever adults get together for some gathering and there are children participating together with them. We call the children to the stage and warmly thank them and the educators. They stand in front of us together with their educators while we applaud and "admire" them, so to say.

– Meaning, they earn social recognition.

– Definitely! How else!? There must be a reward. It is the energy that keeps a person going. If a person is not rewarded, how will he keep on working?

- Suppose I observe things as a specialist (behind the instructor's backs) and I see that a child did something very well and overcame a difficult state. Can I come up to him, compliment him, and say, "Great job, I really liked that!"? Or should I not do that and leave it up to the group?

- You can do that. In fact, I do it myself, too. But the issue with it is that it must be done gently, in a friendly manner, and in a way that doesn't evoke conceit. There is a risk of pride, of making the child feel superior to others because then he might start bossing people around, thinking, "Now I know how things should work around here." It all depends on the preparation, the child, and the circumstances.

- Over the last 100 years psychology has developed a method of becoming aware of and working with "negative" emotions, such as a grudge or a sense of guilt. Is there any point in revealing to a child how this mechanism works so he is able to overcome his touchiness, for example? This is also a behavioral mechanism. If a child knows how it works, perhaps it will be easier for him to get rid of this flaw or use it correctly?

- We definitely discuss and tell children about the reasons why negative emotions arise. But we don't try to abide by today's doctrines because tomorrow those doctrines will change. Instead, we just point out the things that naturally follow from our observations. This is the most important. You do not dictate ready-made formulas for the child, but find them together with him: "Wow! Look at how things happen in life." And together with him you discover his dependence on certain qualities he has and their expressions.

From this standpoint, I really like natural museums where a child can conduct little experiments, watch some phenomenon, set it in motion by himself, and observe the result. Maybe something unpredictable occurs, and then we get an explanation of why this happens in Nature.

Then the child can write this down, and there's a physics lesson for you. You don't need any classes, or to sit in front of a boring teacher, a blackboard, or even a computer screen. This is the best form of learning whenever it is possible. But if it's impossible to do something like that, there are still many scientific movies. But it's best to do it in real life and discuss it afterwards.

THE TRUTH ABOUT LIFE IS NOT THAT SCARY

– Are there any age related rules? For example, should children aged 9–12 be given more information about the animal kingdom, while older children should be told more about social phenomena?

– Of course! That's natural! At every age the same objects are studied differently. Children are more familiar with plants and animals than adults because these things are closer to them. Of course, everything depends on age.

For example, recently we had children visit a factory that produces medicines. This is very interesting! It involves physics, chemistry, biology, and mechanics. It involves processing materials as well as discerning what ingredients are necessary for which medicine, and why.

At first the factory appears like a small building, since pharmaceutical factories are usually not big. Everything there works automatically, with ingredients poured in one by one. Afterwards they are mixed, the pills are churned out, and then they come out prepackaged. Then the workers there tell you about how these medicines are used: which are for headaches and which are for something else. And everything is shown to you in practice.

Children form the right impression from this experience. They immediately understand that there is an enormous amount of professions involved here, integrated in one another, involving mechanics, electronics, chemistry, biology, and so on.

However, this is not suitable for young children. It is more appropriate for a serious teenager.

– We had an interesting case when we asked children ages 9–13 if they wanted to go on an excursion to a prison...

– I was just getting to that. They shouldn't learn only from positive phenomena. We plan on taking children precisely to places like prisons and rehabilitation centers. It definitely must be shown to them, and it has to be done often! Children have to retain impressions from all facets of life, thus forming a distinct attitude.

After all, the whole problem is that the child doesn't feel the implications of his negative actions. If he felt it in advance, then we could treat him like an adult.

Why do we have such a merciful attitude toward children? It's because they cannot see or predict the future. This is why we say that they cannot be held responsible for their actions.

But when a child observes the consequences of someone else's negative actions, such as a person being put in prison, a person being sick, a person who cannot overcome his drug or alcohol addiction, and look what happened to that person: he has lung cancer from smoking, or another person died because he fell off a roof, then we can teach them through the examples of others to "Consider the consequences." In this way we guard them from repeating these actions or mistakes.

We won't start treating them like adults after they see these things. But they will already become adults.

– From what age can we start to involve a child in this process of observing negative things, such as taking them to a children's trauma center where their peers are hospitalized?

– The same age as their hospitalized peers. At age 5 or 6 they will already understand this. "Look at that boy. Let him tell you what he did. Oh, he jumped over a gate, and that one climbed on a rooftop, and that one was run over by a car, and now he's laying there with an injured arm or leg." Do you know what a lesson for life that is!? Of course, we should beware of serious injuries, such as ones where a person loses an eye or an arm. This has to be done very gradually, but they should eventually be shown all of the negative consequences.

And when they get a little bit older, they can visit maternity wards and so on. That is, we have to show them all of life in its proper form. What will this accomplish? This will help them interact correctly and properly place themselves in relation to all of these consequences.

– I think that this is where many parents would ask, "Won't we scare or even paralyze a child with this truth about life?"

– But we aren't just saying to a child out of the blue, "Today let's go on a trip to a hospital and look at broken arms and legs." Our children are in a constant process of upbringing, in a constant process of attainment of themselves and the world, and in a constant discussion of everything around them. That is why we can see the order in which we can show this to them so it would be perceived the right way.

LEARNING TO LIVE FROM LIFE ITSELF

What do we expect from the visits to these places? The children should associate themselves with the person or the phenomenon we show them, both positively and negatively. They should feel involved. Then we will have achieved a positive effect, even by visiting a prison, for example. A person wanted to steal something or to break some law, and this is what happened to him as a result.

– Let's say that children went to a hospital and saw some negative phenomenon. How is this information processed and how are the conclusions drawn?

– Normally, we hold discussions. We come back from the hospital, where we videotaped everything. And we record everything on the same day, so the entire day is devoted to this topic. Also, before the trip we hold a briefing, where we show and tell the children what they will be experiencing. At the hospital, a doctor or a special tour guide explains to us where we are, and what happened to whom. He takes us to see the hospitalized children and tells us how they are being treated and what is happening to them. The children themselves also talk about what happened to them. We record all of this on video and every child takes his own small notes. We even prepare white robes for them, and generally, all of this is done in an attractive, intriguing way.

When we come back, we start discussing this entire process, but from a broader perspective: Why does the hospital exist, how does it work, what do the different doctors specialize in, how do the children get there, and so on.

But most importantly, they also see the benefit of the entire hospital staff, the doctors, nurses, and attendants, as well as the medical drugs, and so on. We show them how humanity depends on various professions and forms of activity, and how all of this comes down to helping people. But on the other hand, they see that a person has to take care of himself so he won't end up in a hospital and become a burden for other people who now have to take care of him.

We have to think about what we can do so we don't become a burden on other people. This is already a correct conclusion: When you want to climb somewhere dangerous, first think about the fact that not only will you break a leg, but other people will have to take care of you. And this is a serious "weight" to carry. This is a good conclusion to make.

TEACHER'S PET

- In the process of interacting with children, someone usually becomes the "teacher's pet." That is, instructors tend to like some children more than others. What's the right way to handle this?

- The instructors cannot do that! If they do, then they are not instructors. Also, we must instill an absolutely integral perception of the group and the world in the children. Someone can't be better than someone else! We were all created the same by Nature, we just have to learn to use our inclinations and qualities correctly. This is a necessary condition for integral interaction. This is what Nature demands of us.

Precisely because we are so different, the connection between us produces such a multifaceted, beautiful world. So we should never cut out anything from a person just because we think it is improper. Under any circumstances, we mustn't tie anyone to a "procrustean bed" of some standard!

The only standard that exists is to give every person the right upbringing. Then he will find his right place in society, and we will have the proper mosaic: a harmonious society.

– So my like or dislike toward someone is just an expression of my own problems?

– No, it shouldn't be there at all! If it is present, that person cannot be an instructor. He has to constantly control himself and work on this.

– How should he work on it?

– He must work on himself individually, as well as with other instructors, to learn to treat the world integrally. Integrally means that in my attitude toward the world, I don't divide people by any external attributes. I initially see them—and myself—as created correctly, and we just have to connect the right way. Then everything will turn out right.

You will see that there is nothing harmful in any person, whatever inclinations he may have, provided they are used correctly. These are the fundamental principles of an integral society, and I think humanity will understand them.

– Is there any point applying groundwork developed by materialistic psychology to a children's– Materialistic psychology naturally lies at the foundation of our approach to the world. We just don't accept its canons as inviolable and sacred. When we start working on the integral upbringing in our groups, we see that new laws, new connections, and new rules emerge. And they, too, change. By studying these laws and connections we gradually develop a new set of rules for a person's behavior in an integral society because we have found ourselves in it involuntarily and don't know its rules. We have to learn to live from life itself.

I hope that humanity will gradually adapt to the new natural laws in which we have found ourselves, and we will try to help anyone who wants to do that.

THE EDUCATOR AS THE STAGE DIRECTOR

- The Changeable Guise of the Educator
- Rotation, Dynamics, and Creativity
- Turn the Whole Surrounding World into a "Mother"
- Should There Be Control Over the Educator?
- The Educator as the Stage Director
- The Age Preceding 9–10 Is Critical
- Children Are the Teachers of the Next Generation
- Parents Should Not Be Educators
- Who Can Be an Educator

Who is the "educator"? How should he be prepared, and how should he interact with children and parents?

– In the regular sense of the word, an educator is one who instructs. Meaning, there are clear instructions and he is in charge of making sure that they are observed to the letter.

However, in our case, we are giving children an upbringing. This means that we do the opposite: We give a person a chance to find everything out on his own, to attain, touch, smell, and taste everything, and then to reach his own conclusion independently. This is what the educator does.

– Even if he's just 3 years older than the child he is working with?

- It doesn't matter. He raises him, he helps him take on a different image, rather than merely carrying out instructions. An instructor is a rigid, military notion, so to say, whereas an educator is a more flexible notion.

THE CHANGEABLE GUISE OF THE EDUCATOR

- If an educator favors some children more than others, should that person not be an educator?

- In that case he has to quickly work on himself (to the best of his ability), or else this group of children should be taken away from him.

Working with children, the educator constantly changes and develops. We are all human, so we all constantly develop. When working with others, even though he has the title of "the educator," he is also "brought up," thanks to them.

If the educator can act in a way where all of his imbalanced or unequal states in relation to the children will turn into an object of work on himself, and he develops a balanced, equal attitude toward everyone, that's a very good thing. However, in truth, this is very difficult. The best way to go about it is to create an environment where his attitude doesn't go through drastic changes in any direction.

- When you describe this kind of educator, I feel that it parallels with my profession. As a psychotherapist, I do not have the right to express sympathy for the people I work with. Otherwise my work will end there. However, I do have a supervisors' group where I get together with people like myself, other psychotherapists. We support each other and work out difficulties that I cannot discuss with my clients. For an educator in the integral system, is there a group of educators like himself in which he can figure out his questions?

– Educators get together at meetings. They constantly study in order to elevate themselves higher and higher, and to discuss questions and solve them among each other. Additionally, they constantly study all kinds of source texts and thus advance. Besides working with children, they have to attune themselves in the right direction. Only once they do that can they come into the children's group.

Before an educator comes to the group, he has to read, listen, and delve into some new materials. In other words, he must attune himself. He can't just wake up and walk into the environment of children. He has to take on a specific guise, create it inside of him, and only then come in. This requires preparation and fine-tuning each and every time. And this fine-tuning usually happens among a group of educators, teachers, and instructors.

– What is the guise he has to wear?

– It's the image of a person who is a guiding system. It's as if he's not a person, but a system that forms a "semi finished product" out of every child.

The educator must constantly think about how to "tweak" the child and guide him in the needed direction through opposite questions, positive or negative influences, through others, and with the help of the collective's influence on every person.

He shouldn't just manipulate a child automatically. Rather, he should constantly seek the best way for the child to act according to the choice of a specific goal: This is how I have to connect with others; this is how I have to position myself.

Most important, they should accumulate as many behavioral models as possible—the most multifaceted and contradicting ones, positive and negative, the most diverse ones.

After that, through discussion, games, and socializing with one another they should understand which model is best suited for you to sympathize with, to wear, and to remain in. One should bring oneself to a state where everyone is equal, and then choose the necessary image that accords with that vision.

ROTATION, DYNAMICS, AND CREATIVITY

– Previously we said that ideally, a group should consist of eight to ten children at most, with not one, but two or even three instructors working with them.

– I think that a group of ten children with two instructors is the optimal set up.

– Should one of the instructors always be with the children or should they alternate?

– I think they should alternate. Of course, children feel more comfortable with one instructor, but getting used to things limits them, creating standards that are perpetuated from one day to the next. Instead, we should constantly "pull the rug" from under the young person's feet so he constantly has to piece his world together like a puzzle. This will make his orientation more accurate. He will have to figure out in which direction and in what way he should position himself with friends and with instructors, and how he should act under the new circumstances.

That is, we have to bring him up to be as flexible as possible, and permanent instructors do not cater to this issue.

I think that with many educators in a large group simultaneously, it can feel that way. But still, this is a rather limited space. The best approach is for everything to change all the time, including the setting, the mixture of children, and the instructor that's next to each of them.

– How many instructors are we talking about in this rotation? Is it ten people or is it a new person every time the children meet?

– The most important thing is that they alternate. It's best to have four pairs of educators who constantly alternate in a group of ten children. They move from one group to another, and these pairs change, as well.

Then there will be sufficient alternation of the setting, and the dynamics will be observed. Additionally, the children's group mixes, as well.

They have to feel that all of us—all the people on Earth—are participating in a single, integral, global community. And I don't care who exactly is next to me, I have to be able to understand everyone and to establish a relationship with all.

There must be as few boundaries as possible, whether qualitative, quantitative, temporary, or human ones. The topics must constantly change, as well. Absolutely everything must change!

That way a person will feel how there are constant changes happening within him. He will be forced to constantly reevaluate the setting, himself, and others, to revisit the criteria that previously seemed clear and correct, and to which he has already grown accustomed. Habit is not good. There must be non-stop creativity.

– You have just essentially suggested to remove all of the resources on which pedagogy relies.

– That's because it's easier for the pedagogues. They build a stagnant setting or system for themselves because they feel comfortable in it. But what room for creativity does that leave?

– In that case, where will a child get resources? From this general system?

– Yes. How else can it work? There are seven billion people around me and I have to feel comfortable being together with all of them. I have to be willing to absorb all of their images within me.

If I am willing to do that with just a small team, then I will never come out of my home, playground, or kindergarten. In principle, this is what is happening to people today. They experience pleasant things in their childhood, and sometimes in their later youth (although by then their circle of friends becomes considerably narrower), and then they don't want to go anywhere.

Why is the "Classmates.com" network so popular? What are people drawn to? They don't have anything! That's why they only want to return to their playgrounds and schools. Why? It's because there they had boundaries and felt good. "So let's become children again," they think. In other words, they are still children. They never grew up. And they did not receive any tools for entering the world and finding their bearings in it.

But what are the attributes by which I choose my friends at "Classmates.com"? When I was young, I was friends with them. But today I am grown up and I don't have anyone. So, I'll go back to them.

Where have we arrived? Essentially, a person never left childhood and he misses it. But what kind of childhood was it? It was also limited by the boundaries of a rigid system. The system did not teach him to be flexible, so he wants to at least return to it in order to feel comfortable. He is a small cube in a small box, and feels good there.

– For the first three years of a child's life, he is next to his mother and is in close contact with her. Suddenly, a drastic change occurs as the child begins to mingle with others. How can we make this transition comfortable?

– It has been preplanned by Nature. We see how suddenly, at age three, a child starts playing with others. Previously he did not even feel the existence of others. All he had was himself, his mother, and his toy. That was it; he didn't have any social drives.

But then he starts to feel, "I want to play with someone," "I want to look at that person and learn to do something together." He begins to observe other children. This happens automatically and we start to develop this drive as soon as it appears.

TURN THE WHOLE SURROUNDING WORLD INTO A "MOTHER"

- A child has a need to keep returning to the same place. He plays somewhere on neutral territory and then he wants to come back, to immerse himself in that sensation again. Adults also do that.

- We want to return to our mothers. This is natural. It is instilled in our nature. But how can we make the environment, which constantly expands around us, become our "mom"? Even though it expands and absorbs more and more foreign images into it, how can we make it remain as friendly, loving, and comfortable to us as the womb in which we developed and which we continue to long for, similar to how a child runs to his mom and wants to hide under her skirt?

We have to learn how to turn the surrounding environment into a "womb." If we create an environment that has the qualities of bestowal and love, it will be just like a mother.

In principle, this is what the great commandment, "Love your neighbor as yourself," talks about. You were instinctively made to feel what a mother is—the safest, kindest place in the world. You might already be a grownup, but you still instinctively aspire to this feeling just like a child.

So make the world be like that!

- People really do long for it. What you are describing sounds wonderful, but it seems unrealistic.

– That means we have to think about how to make it happen. Besides, our nature obligates us to achieve this anyhow. The world is now starting to be revealed as an integral, global system. What does that mean? It means that the world is forcing us to treat each other the same as our mothers treated us. Then, together we will acquire precisely this state of being "in the mother's womb."

– Are you saying that the globalization that scares people is actually a "large, loving mom" coming our way?

– This is a revolution, and how we go through it depends entirely on us. We can either go through it by the good path and joint efforts, understanding where we are going, or we will go through it completely disorientated, like a child who has lost its mother. Nature will force us to create a society that corresponds exactly to the image of our mother, Nature, "Mother Nature."

– Usually, mothers take it very hard when a child acquires independence, when his need to be next to her diminishes.

– In the ideal upbringing, when a child starts wishing to separate from the mother, to the extent that he desires it, he should build a surrounding environment (with our help), which replaces his mother, and gradually transfer her function to the society around him.

Nature has arranged things so a child will separate from the mother. This is inevitable. We just have to make the surrounding world replace the mother for every child, but precisely to the degree that the child has the right attitude toward the surrounding world.

A mother accepts her child however he is. He is hers. And to the world, he is "the world's" or "not the world's" depending on how correctly he treats the world. We have to create an environment that teaches the child the right attitude toward the world. Then the world will replace his mother for him.

The mother is the mother for the child's body, while the world is the mother of the human being in a person, when he forms the right image out of himself. To the degree that he is "not yet a person," meaning to the extent that he does not live in bestowal and love for others, the world will relate toward him differently, not as a mother.

– One of the definitions of a psychological disorder is hypersensitivity to oneself and a lack of sensitivity to the outside world. If we create this structure, will we raise healthy children in that sense?

– Most importantly, they will be healthy in the spiritual sense. And naturally, it will be expressed in their physical well-being.

SHOULD THE EDUCATOR BE MONITORED?

– We said that the educator has to attune himself to the general interaction. And it's unacceptable to prefer some children to others. But still, what if these feelings still arise?

– The educator has to rise above himself. Otherwise, he isn't an educator. The educator should only work with the collective. He does not have any personal feelings or opinions.

He only steps forward as a stabilizer or a deliberate destabilizer in this environment. He has a clear direction and objective by which he acts. He is like a machine that works only to develop the participants in the team or the group, without switching on any desires of his own.

– When a person is in an unpleasant state, he tries to ignore it, to suppress it. Taking this into account, is it necessary to monitor the educator?

– Naturally. In our groups, where we conduct research and develop techniques, everything is videotaped. This lets us observe the dynamics that exist there. The instructors talk about the problems they encounter within them or in the group, but still there are some things we see from the side, and some things we don't. It is a process.

However, the instructor quickly finds his bearings in this practice. It is simple and does not require any "clever" theories, and originates from integrity, globality, unity, connection, and flexibility.

What operates here is a person's natural aspiration. And that is something that does not require many theories or methods. The educator grasps the necessary methods very quickly. He lives in them, finds his way around them, and becomes sensitive to them. He starts to acquire his own techniques and feels how to attune children better to the right mode of interaction with each other. There is a lot of room for variations, searches, and states. In the process of doing this, one feels how by studying our nature, we manipulate ourselves and Nature in order to bring ourselves to unity, which is the goal.

– Do educators get together in order to watch the videos with their participation and discuss it with others? Is there room for constructive criticism?

– The educators should also have their own group, in which they can discuss everything with each other. They have to study every person's experience as well as their joint experience, materials, and impressions. After all, why should every person make the same mistakes? If something happened in one group, they should try to model it in another and see what happens there. They should treat this process as current and alive, and understand that as children are like play dough, so are we.

Let's try it. No harm can be done. Everything is under our control, and if we try it out on ourselves, we will gain impressions of what is right and what is wrong, and this is a valuable experience that we need.

Progress in a collective must include the sensation of being immersed in negative images, phenomena, connections, and conflicts. We must constantly learn from them.

Positive things grow only over the negative, after we experience and discern them. We have to feel our nature to its full negative depth. Only then will we be able to build something positive atop it.

THE EDUCATOR AS THE STAGE DIRECTOR

– If an educator becomes so involved in the children's environment, then he literally merges with it. Won't it be a problem if he becomes the same as the kids, a degradation for the educator?

– I don't think it is a degradation. A person who raises children has to be on the level of the children. If he constantly controls himself, bringing them to a specific state, then he is on the level of the educator and on the level of the children simultaneously.

He has to retain these two levels within him and clearly understand: This is me and this is them. How do I manipulate them? How do I make them control themselves? How do I make them become aware of their behaviors, their natures, and their inclinations? Where do they have to rise, and above what? How can they overcome themselves, and for what, for which goals?

He is always with them, analyzing what is happening and experiencing all the states along with them. But he is present there as a stage director or producer. He molds the group using conflicting states, even ones that are artificial. By fabricating all sorts of problems for them, he evokes greater convergence between them.

After all, the entire group works on compatibility, although the children might be very different. For example, new children might enter the group, or the instructors might change, things may become strained, or some interruptions might occur and problems may arise.

We constantly place the children in these situations and see how they resolve them, how they find "a common denominator" in every situation.

The educator has to be the stage director or the producer of this process, and he has to do it dynamically, constantly maintaining control of it.

– Should the children feel that the educator is on those two levels?

– Yes, of course, they have to understand that. He is with them, but he knows and understands more than they do.

Actually, I don't see any difference between the role of an instructor, educator, a teacher, or a professional who regulates the behavior of masses or crowds, who controls society, a nation, or even humanity. In principle, this is the same profession. It's just that in the first case there is a small group of children whom I am raising, and in the latter case there is a large group of people, and I also have to raise them.

How can we reach adults, the masses, or the crowd? I don't think that there is a big difference between an instructor in a small group and a person who needs to control large numbers of people, meaning not to control, but to raise them.

THE AGE PRECEDING 9–10 IS CRITICAL

– Say we have gathered children of different ages in one place where they have to learn to find a "common denominator" in different situations. We gather an entire hall of children together, say, 500 or 1,000 children of different ages. How should we interact with them?

– You are starting with a mass right away, but that is incorrect.

We see how a child develops naturally: First he is in the mother's womb, then he is next to her, then he crawls several feet away from the mother, then takes a few steps further, and then moves several more feet away from her in the apartment. Then he goes out into the surrounding world, but he is still next to her, in a stroller or in a baby wrap (depending on the culture).

We see that a child gradually gains access to the environment, only to the extent of his ability to interact with it correctly. That is how he expands his circle.

The same thing should happen here. You cannot just put 1,000 children together and expect to be able to handle them properly. This is impossible.

The only thing you'll be able to do is suppress them. You can sit them down, turn out the lights, and place a screen in front of them so they'll watch some animated movie. But this is not upbringing, and you don't achieve anything by doing that. You merely detach them from themselves. But upbringing has to be built on expansion.

If you already have groups of children who understand one another, who are able to unite as one, then you can try to connect several groups together. Then three of four groups will be like three or four children together.

You can do this once they already have a common understanding with one another, once you have completed the preliminary work with every child in every group so they feel this togetherness within them.

– What can you say about age boundaries?

- By age 9 or 10, a person's foundation is instilled entirely. Entirely! After age 9 or 10 you only develop what has been instilled in him consciously and unconsciously, including instincts and genetic information. Everything that is already in him develops from here on, but practically nothing is added.

There has to be a very precise plan about how to behave with children during the period when they are accumulating their initial impressions from the surrounding world, which happens prior to age 9-10, at the oldest. After that it is very difficult to do anything with a child.

Of course, he will imitate our norms of behavior and rules. But this will be like instructions rather than something that's personally his. It won't be the same as how he gradually absorbs an attitude to the world from you, making it his own, right after being born and in the process of growing up. If he learns about something for the first time after age 9 or 10, it won't be his own anymore.

- Let me clarify. If we prepare a child from early childhood and he goes through specific states, then by age 9 he should already have experience uniting into large groups?

- He has to understand why this is done. He has to acquire specific skills in this area. He has to feel positive and negative sensations, contacts, actions, and results on his level of understanding, perception, and instincts.

We have to collect all of this and accumulate all of these images in him. They have to be present in him like data: I am together with everyone; I am against everyone; this is good; this is bad. They have to accumulate in him like frames in a chronological sequence.

Then, he will use these frames in his life. These models will be constantly present in him as both conscious and unconscious reference points. They will be constantly operating in him, and he will orient himself with their help, often without being aware that he is doing it.

It is necessary to fill him with positive and negative impressions about unity, globality, and integrality from the earliest age, as much as possible. This will be his ticket to the new world.

CHILDREN ARE THE TEACHERS OF THE NEXT GENERATION

– Should the educator interact with the children's parents?

– It's preferable for the same setting and attitude to continue at home. Unfortunately, this is only possible if the parents also go through this system of upbringing. Otherwise they simply won't know what is required of them.

They will mechanically place some boundaries, the child will feel how artificial they are, and will think that his parents don't understand anything. He will be much more internally flexible than them. He will be socially wiser and will have a better understanding of society, human relations, motivations, goals, and mindset. This wisdom will keep developing in him even if we stop providing him with psychological nuances and methods.

If the parents don't develop alongside the child, he will view them as merely "animals" [belonging to the animate degree of development]. One's attitude toward society and one's ability to create the right environment are what differentiate a person from an animal.

– Suppose parents study the method of integral upbringing on their own level to some extent.

– They have to go through our courses before they even start planning on having children. And that doesn't apply just to parents. In principle, all people must go through it: young, old, and children. But it's especially important for those who plan on becoming parents. Are they planning to give birth to a human being of the future, or just a "cub"?

- So do we have to develop courses for people who did not go through all of these phases in childhood? Is it possible to prepare them now?

- Only through the media, especially internet and television. There are no other means. Print materials are becoming practically extinct, leaving internet and television as the most important means of communication.

We have to understand that all of humanity is on the threshold of a new world and needs to go through a buffer period in its upbringing, its education, so they can be learning while adapting to it.

Soon there won't be anything else for us to do. We won't have the raw materials to produce everything we are producing today just to throw out what we buy six months later. People will gradually start devoting more and more time to organizing these educational establishments, so I am certain that the most important profession in the next generation will be an educator, an instructor, or a teacher. But first, they have to be properly trained for it.

I hope that the children who are currently studying in our groups will become the first teachers of the future generation.

PARENTS SHOULD NOT BE EDUCATORS

- Say there are parents who take the course, study this method, and have a child who goes to this school. Can you depict how this family will interact with each other? A child comes home after spending most of his day in an environment of peers. What should his interaction be like with his parents and grandparents?

Where is the child's place? Where are the brothers and sisters? How do you envision it?

– Children aren't drawn to their parents or to their grandparents. They are drawn to their peers or to their personal activities. They need grandparents in the capacity of an environment that helps them and services them, but nothing more than that.

Therefore, I think that there won't be any problems in this area and the parents don't even have to go through a certain kind of upbringing. What needs to be achieved here is for them not to interfere. They should not be raising the children.

They just have to provide the right reaction so a child will understand that no matter where he is, he is always in an environment that helps him, and constantly demands a specific type of development from him, the right type of understanding and interaction with the surrounding environment. Nothing else is required of them. Parents should not be educators.

The reason for this is that upbringing happens in an environment of people who are like you, with whom you are equal, and with whom you constantly interact. Parents are perceived as something high and big, as something that serves you, protects you, and takes care of you. Therefore, they are not considered educators.

Development occurs in a large social environment, not in a small corner where the only people around are my mom, my dad, and me. This is good only up to age 2.

– But suppose a child comes home upset because something bad happened. How should the parents react to that?

– I don't think that the parents can truly understand the child's state and offer the correct analysis of what is happening. This is something he has to do in a group, through debate and discussion.

We have to approach the world realistically. We are not living in the corrected world yet, where a child is immediately admitted into the correct process of development at home and everywhere else he goes. We are still not in that situation.

Ideally, all problems must be resolved in the place where they emerge, in the same circle of children where he is brought up. He shouldn't have any other environments at all.

– But what should the parents do? I also have children and I know that when my child comes home upset, I want to hug him and comfort him. Can I do that? Or is that incorrect?

– Why comfort him? You shouldn't do that, but you can hug him. When you meet a person who's close to you, you hug him. This is natural.

However, I think we will attain a level of communication where we won't feel the need to sense each other through touch. Our inner sensations and ability to feel one other will intensify to a point where the body will not be a necessary organ or means of contact.

– That's difficult to imagine because in the meantime it is a source of tremendous pleasure.

– For now everything passes through the body because we have no other sensations besides it. But when we gradually develop towards coming out of ourselves and connecting with others, towards perceiving the world through others, the body recedes and I begin to feel my direct connection and inclusion in others. My image becomes included in the image of others and simultaneously becomes an image that I share with them.

Then joint sensations emerge, but they are no longer bodily sensations that I have to hug others or let them taste what I am eating, or when we have to participate in a meal together and exchange some kind of physical contact. Rather, a completely new kind of contact emerges, even in the sexual sense. That is, everything grows into a completely different realm of sensations, combinations, and connections with one another, to a point where our world on the animate level loses its importance. This is what will gradually happen. Of course, it is still ahead of us and it's unrealistic to talk about it right now, but I want to indicate the direction in which we are headed.

– We definitely have to know about this. Do you know why am I so interested in the parents? It's because most of the questions about the method are coming from them. One of the parents' functions is to provide their child with safety.

– This is the most important thing, and it's the same with animals. The only thing that guides them is the safety of their offspring.

– Influenced by this very important need, parents want to find out more about what is happening to their child in these courses, how he interacts in this environment, and so on.

– Their child is constantly filmed by cameras so they can watch everything from home. And not only they. We are currently practicing this at our education center. We have many groups all over the world in our system of upbringing. Some of the groups are primary, meaning they conduct constant work, discussions, and research on themselves. They constantly film themselves and show this material to everyone else. You can go on the internet, type in the URL, and watch a specific group and what it is doing at any moment.

There are specific hours when our primary groups, in which we conduct the main work, simply broadcast everything happening at their location. And the other groups sit and watch, listen, and study this live experience in their locations.

- Still, I would like to ask about the parents again. Suppose a father and a mother watched one of the videos...

- They can watch their beloved child non-stop, 24 hours a day.

- But can they participate in some way?

- We don't practice this yet. That would require an additional system of interaction between the parents and children, and I think this will be possible in the future. However, I like to talk only about what is currently feasible and what will be feasible in the near future. I think that the system of interaction between parents and children will not be set up in the immediate future. We haven't the opportunity to accomplish this yet.

So how can they participate? For that they would have to be on the level of the educators. And what does "participating" mean? If they cannot detach from their personal "I" and control themselves, how can they take part in the upbringing?

- Still, we can give parents some practical advice. For example, when a child comes home, should the parents state their point of view in some way?

- The upbringing should not be continued at home. What's required of the parents is to be gentle, caring, and loving, and that's all. They should not be raising the child. They have to give him simple, animate, bodily support, provide him with the amount of confidence that he needs, and that's all. I don't think that it's the parents' job to turn a child into a human being. Only the surrounding environment can do that. Only society can make a person because a person is part of the society.

Parents cannot create an environment around him or an image that would enable him to become a person. By trying, they will simply cause him to remain a big child forever. This is what we often see today, how a grown man who's 40 years old cannot separate from his mother.

WHO CAN BE AN EDUCATOR

– Do the educator's personal talents or level of preparation matter? Who can be an educator, and who shouldn't be one?

– This is a very important question. First of all, an educator has to be brought up himself in a way that enables him to rise above himself and any of his personal qualities, meaning to be as objective as possible in his interaction with the children.

Of course, none of the children should be good or bad in his eyes, or attractive or unattractive. You know very well how much this influences our attitude toward children. The educator cannot view anyone as intelligent or stupid, and so on. He has to treat everyone only from the viewpoint of their growth: How can I help each of them be spiritually, morally, physically, and most important—socially healthy?

The educator has to be grateful to the children because they enable him to grow. They provide him with a bountiful environment to constantly work on himself and perfect his level of spiritual growth together with them. After all, working on oneself is the most wonderful activity.

The educator must hold constant discussions with other educators and continually expand his knowledge in the method of integral, global upbringing. He has to be in this system of learning and self-study 24 hours a day.

It is very important for him to be in a society of educators who care only about this, who influence him, and constantly strive to turn every child into a human being, just like him. At the same time, this society must influence him in a way that will turn him into a human being.

That is, he has to be a person who is constantly growing spiritually and morally, and for whom spiritual development is the goal of his life.

In principle, this is the goal of our existence; it is the goal for everyone, the entire human society. This is the task that Nature has given us. This is the challenge it poses to our generation, and the educator must simply make all of this happen in practice.

Of course, his personal qualities are important. Children need to have educators with a variety of qualities and external expressions. The children have to perceive these expressions very vividly and tangibly, and discern them, realizing that the educators are not some machines that are somewhere over there. Rather, the educators have to be outstanding individuals.

At a certain point we begin to mingle children with adults so the children can adapt to the adults, and not only to their peers. Then the educators simply merge with the surrounding, external environment.

At least once or twice a week we should hold events where children and adults unite. When the children participate in these events along with the adults, they begin to understand them better, to accept them, and to see that adults support them, as well, giving them a place and making room for the children to express themselves just like adults among adults.

WE GROW BY PLAYING

Another topic that I would like to discuss is games that are played by children and adults. A few decades ago Johan Huizinga, a cultural historian and philosopher, published a book titled, *Homo Ludens* (*Man the Player*), which became a kind of a cult-book. After its publication, people started talking a lot about the role of games in the development of man and life in general. So what is a "game"?

– The extensive influence of games on human development has been known since ancient times. We like to play. And practically speaking, we spend most of our lives playing. Even my pre-dissertation examination in philosophy included a question on games.

Games are everywhere, including in math and in Nature. Games have a very important role in the development of animals and even

91

plants. The element of playing is present in any transformation, in any forward movement from one state to another.

– Nevertheless, there is a notion that games are related only to childhood, and when a person grows up it's inappropriate for him to play because he has to be more serious.

– Unfortunately, there is indeed such a notion. But of course, this is a dull perception of the world. When a person stops playing, he stops developing.

FIVE ATTRIBUTES OF A GAME

– Every game has five attributes or fixed characteristics. The first characteristic of a game is that one is free and participates in it voluntarily. Huizinga wrote that a game is freedom.

In the integral method, we are talking about a group of children. How can we set things up so their actions are voluntary? Can a child join a game and leave it at will, or not?

– "Voluntary and free" refers to the choice of one's actions and deeds until the person (whether a child or an adult) becomes certain that he is acting according to his conviction, the analysis he has made, and the decision he has reached. As long as he is not certain about the next move, he doesn't do it.

And when he acts in life, or "makes a move," just as in a game, he clearly knows that he is doing it himself. He has reached this conclusion on his own and is acting this way on his own.

– So this is the first attribute: doing it voluntarily and having the freedom to enter and leave.

Second: a game is always "make-believe." A child has to know that it's a game.

Third, a game has a spatial zone and a time, meaning there is a beginning and an end to the game, and certain spatial boundaries.

Fourth, a game always comes with rules.

Fifth and last: What's important is the process of the game, while the result of the game is secondary. Huizinga even said that as soon as a result appears in a game, it stops being a game.

– If the result is set in advance, it limits the freedom of choice.

– You have said that there are games in the animate kingdom and even in plants. Could you explain?

– We observe the elements of a game even on the level of cellular development, the development of organisms, and within living organisms.

No growth or development is possible without the presence of several possibilities. There always has to be a specific choice that is played out and made, and this choice is always made through playing. This can be explained using the probability theory, mathematical theory, and others. Meaning, we see that Nature is playing.

LIFE IS A GAME

– For some reason I just recalled a chance game that used to be popular. Where does the hope that people hang on games of chance come from?

– When we cannot know exactly what the right decision is, we put ourselves in the hands of fate, hoping that there is a destiny, an unpredictable upper force that controls us, and we give ourselves over to it. Of course, in games we don't take it seriously.

In life, however, we see that even when we plan ahead and want everything to go according to our plan, things unfold by different laws. That's where a discrepancy between common sense, my established dogmas, and what really happens in life emerges.

How can I leave my dogmas and merge with the actions that are actually happening outside of me, under the influence of some external, higher force of Nature?

Humanity is entering a state of integral, global governance by Nature. Previously we did not notice it, but developed through the generations according to our egoism, changing ourselves, society, and the social orders.

But today we—individualists, egoists—are starting to find ourselves in a completely different format. We are included in a mechanism that operates integrally, like an analog system where all the parts are completely interconnected, mutually determining each other's state, and no one has any free movement. A person influences the whole world with his thoughts and desires, not to mention the physical actions. This is called "the butterfly effect."

There is a contradiction between how we were created, how we map out the world based on our nature, and how Nature actually works in reality. A discrepancy arises between the two systems. And that is when the desire to play emerges.

To play means to give yourself over to the will of the integral nature that controls us, which we cannot understand, and with which we cannot act in unison. Therefore, a person seems to give himself over to a force, a governance that comes from Nature. In a sense, he throws a dice, thinking, "The result does not depend on me. I am simply giving myself over to the whim of chance." So what should we do?

If we tried to "team up" with Nature, we would win. Of course, we wouldn't be thoughtlessly "throwing dice," but we would try to penetrate the integral governance. And even though it contradicts our common sense, if we would try to come closer to this integral governance, we would see that sometimes it's worthwhile to act in that integral manner, that the advantage of doing that is obvious.

– If we take a regular, traditional game, immediately a stereotype arises, the idea that it is a competition, and in the end one side will win and the other will lose.

When you talk about "winning" the global, integral game, what do you mean? What is the objective and result of this game?

– The objective is not to act in a way that is doomed to fail because it is totally disconnected from the actions that are instilled in Nature, and which Nature will carry out anyhow.

If we act in even a slightly different direction from Nature, we will suffer to the extent of our deviation from Nature's program. If I deviate 10 degrees from Nature's integral law of development, or if I stray 20 or 30 degrees, then there will be earthquakes, tsunamis, hurricanes, financial catastrophes, or even wars.

If we started studying ourselves in relation to the integral governance under which we exist today, we could prevent many catastrophes and would gradually learn to feel and analyze our actions, to discern whether they are desirable or not. An old maxim says, "If you don't know how to act, its best if you sit and don't act at all," because by acting without knowing how, you stray from the right course, whereas by not acting, you just passively flow with the movement.

PLAYING BY THE RULES

– Rules are very important in any game. Can you describe the rules of this global, integral game?

– In technology there is a concept of an "integral, analog" system, where the entrance and exit are connected through the whole system and all of its parts are completely interconnected like cogwheels in a closed mechanism.

As we develop, the bond between us is becoming more and more rigid. In the past we were able to "slip through holes" in some way and attach our little wheels to one another only slightly. But today we are moving into a state where every person is necessarily spinning in a rigid clutch with others, thus determining whether humanity will move in a favorable or unfavorable direction.

Therefore, if we map out our lives less according to our egoism and in a more integrated manner, we would reach a common conclusion that it is necessary to create a joint system of governance, a world government that will unite all of our operations into a single system. That way we would achieve greater understanding of this integral system and would prevent many catastrophes.

We see the tremendous shifts occurring in the world today, such as the revolutions in the Near and Middle Eastern countries, and not only there. That is how a world government gradually forms. Life is forcing us toward it. But it would be better if everything happened in a more humane way and the approach toward that government would be more orderly.

– If we suppose that man plays and acts by the laws of Nature, then who will be opposite to him?

– A corrected person is opposite to an egoist. First of all, it is necessary to act less egoistically.

Today any game of protectionism leads to horrible consequences. It's as if you're spinning the cogwheels in the opposite direction. This is first of all detrimental to yourself. That is why it is necessary to somehow stop this isolated, egoistic movement of every person in his own direction. The world has to be convinced that cooperation is necessary. And today we can do that.

What does this cooperation mean? We have to bring the whole world to follow the global decisions. But first let's start by getting closer! Let's imagine that there is no South America with its dictators, no Eastern rulers, no USA or Russia, no Europe, and no China with its exploding population, but we are all in one global, integral country. Today we have the power to do that because we depend on each other economically, politically, and especially for provision of raw materials. We can reach that state of cooperation, and then involve the game element.

– You just touched on a question that is directly connected with upbringing. My generation was raised to believe that if you don't like something or can't do something, you have to try harder and eventually you will achieve. But what you're describing sounds quite different. So do I have to make efforts or should I stop and look around to see where I am and what I should do next?

– Most of our actions lead to opposite results, so we shouldn't keep trying, thus causing more damage. First, we must discern whether or not we are in harmony with Nature. That is, to what extent does Nature support our plans and actions? Then we have to ask ourselves: "What is required of us?"

We develop under the influence of the inner drives that Nature instills in us, which we just realize. Wouldn't it be better to first discover what plans are inherent in our natural development, and then build ourselves according to them?

Nature can develop us mercifully or harshly, depending on how we position ourselves. This favorable positioning is our first task.

– In many of the games we know, besides the players there is an objective character, a referee. If we are talking about integral, global games, is there a referee there, someone who acts more objectively than us?

– It would be nice if this was an assembly of researchers, serious scientists, sociologists, political scientists, and economists who would work together. That's because we constitute one, single system in which everything is interconnected. We understand that decisions cannot be made by force. I think that today it is clear to everyone. Notions of power structures that can single-handedly decide, govern, and execute, are falling apart. Therefore, there has to be a referee, a serious research group that offers its decisions and solutions after observing what is happening, and which can truly compare society with Nature, discern the mistakes, and provide evaluations, making our subsequent actions more correct.

PLAYING UNTIL WE ACHIEVE TOTAL EQUIVALENCE WITH NATURE

– According to game theory, the most important component of a game is the rules. Should these rules be fixed or should they be subject to change?

– They constantly change because we constantly delve deeper into ourselves and into the surrounding world, constantly discovering ourselves as globally connected on deeper layers. Nature is integral and global on its every level; there is not a single atom in the universe that does not evoke changes in the entire universe whenever it changes. This globality is total. The problem is that we still cannot feel this system, and therefore cannot govern the human society.

Can you imagine that the ideal state that Nature has set for us is one where any movement we make—physical, integral, on the level of desires or in our minds—must be in total harmony with the entire universe!? It's simply inconceivable what we have to reach, how we have to experience Nature at the end of our development. But Nature will bring us to that.

Comparing ourselves to this global, integral nature, and continuously moving toward it contains an element of play because there is a lot that we don't know. We don't know our next step. We have to somehow anticipate it, and act it out. Maybe we can act it out and somehow implement it in our society, possibly in parts of society where we are studying this phenomenon that we want to introduce into our immediate environment or into the general human society.

There are many game elements like that, which pertain more to research than to a game. But research is also kind of a game. And since we are studying Nature and ourselves on increasingly deeper levels, since the integral nature is becoming increasingly clearer, the game is constant all the way through total equivalence with Nature, a state that we cannot imagine today.

However, we can suppose that this is what Nature has enacted and instilled, and that this is where Nature is leading us. Apparently, egoism was deliberately created in man, to make it possible for him to play, meaning to develop, all the way to the point of understanding, awareness, adaptation, and even participation in the governance of this entire, integral nature.

– Are there any qualities or characteristics in behavior that can revoke this opportunity and prevent one from developing?

– If he doesn't agree; if he opposes the integral system. And we will see this very quickly, first in the example of countries whose regime brutally suppresses people's ability to develop integrally.

What does "integral development" mean? At this stage, fundamentalist regimes seem closer to actualizing integration because they unite society, leading people under their slogan, symbol, or flag. At a certain point along the way, they might appear more successful and more corresponding to integration, at least within their specific country. But afterwards they will start positioning themselves against everyone else, against the more global government. At that point they will naturally start crumbling. Their destruction will evoke enormous changes, their inner reconstruction. As a result, every fundamentalist regime and society will come in conscious contact with its own people and with others. And because these regimes are egoistic— yet internally connected with their egos—on the one hand they'll appear to be working in companionship, seemingly in a form that matches Nature. But on the other hand, their bonding will be only to succeed in destroying others, which makes them opposite from Nature. For this reason we'll see them having short-lived success, where the bonding between them prevails, but eventually, we will see their ruin once their opposition from Nature manifests.

We should study these phenomena, but from the viewpoint of every part and everyone as a whole coming closer to global unity.

"THE GOOD BABYLON"—AN INTERNET GAME

- If we look at the integral, global society in the process of evolution, then the playing zone also goes through gradual development, from the scope of a room to the whole world.

- If only we could create that kind of game system on the internet and offer it to all of humanity! In this game, the reward would be good prizes or honors, things that attract all of us, who are little egoists. Let's create a single human society, and call this game "Babylon." But not Babylon in the negative sense of the word, but in the positive one.

This will be a game of cooperation. And it has to involve egoistic problems that gradually appear on all levels—emotional, personal, familial, between people, and between civilizations. It should include struggles over sources of food, raw materials, wealth, knowledge, fame, and power. And the people playing this game will have to find the solutions to these problems. Specialists, including psychologists, will add as many elements as possible into this game, meaning they will model it to evoke real emotions in people.

The game will gradually turn into a theater where the player will start playing the role of an integral part of society. Albeit virtual for now, he will already feel the involuntary changes happening to him and will see the positive results of this game in the real world. He will see how he and the space around him become kinder, safer, and more comfortable. In fact, this game could be turned into a system of integral upbringing.

I hope that a game like that will appear on the internet. That is why it is called "Inter-net"—a worldwide, universal system that connects everyone.

– I don't like computer games, but this one got me interested.

– It is an opportunity for us to create a person, to mold him! And he will do it on his own! By participating in this game, he will start seeing the opportunities to change himself for the sake of attaining a specific goal while receiving rewards "along the way," including approval and respect, meaning everything that can help him move forward.

If an adult plays this game, children will see how he succeeds and how it pushes him forward. Or, vice versa, if the players are children who become successful at the game, the parents will be happy about it and will show them their approval. We have to use egoism correctly to move toward integration.

Look at all the internet communities! It's all a game! So why don't we make this kind of game? But we have to make it productive and aim it in a direction where it brings benefit.

This kind of game will create a new type of individual who involuntarily sees precisely how he has to play in life. After all, we know that our actions change us.

– Then we won't have the problem of taking the children off the computer. We won't need to.

– A child will take part in this and this will be his environment! Under the influence of this environment, every one of us will be able to try himself out.

And because globality and integrality will gradually become expressed in this system, through it we will be able to work out our subsequent behavioral models. I can turn to this game as if to an expert on the next steps I have to make, and as a result, I will make less mistakes.

It might seem like I am creating a game, but in reality I am creating a model of the correct society. If I move around there like a game chip, placing myself in specific levels, actions, qualities, changes, and communication, then I can see where I will succeed and where I won't ahead of time. After all, the laws of the integral society, which gradually manifest in this system, will give me the right reaction, either negative or positive. That is how I will choose the best possible movement toward my goal of balance with the entire system, toward my most comfortable state.

– And what is the center of this balanced system? How can I tell that I am moving precisely towards the center?

– That's easy: I feel better there than anywhere else. On the one hand, I feel absolutely free, and on the other hand, absolutely connected to everyone, which gives me even greater freedom.

It's astounding how by experiencing conflicting situations and influences, I feel that I am locked in a loop with all the other cogwheels, spinning along with them, since we are in one coherent game. We experience mutual pleasure, mutual expansion, attainment, understanding, and enjoyment. I receive everything and I don't conceal anything from anyone. I enjoy being in harmony with others and bestowing upon them.

It's just as in a ball game where the passes create the state of a game between us, where we interact with each other the right way. The same thing happens here, but to the full extent and on all levels, including animate and human. I begin to experience myself in the state of a global, integral, and wonderful game. Streams of communications flow through me just like a ball is passed in a game. We experience the pleasure of playing the game precisely in this harmony.

A FLIGHT ABOVE THE UNIVERSE

– You have repeatedly mentioned how important it is for a person to come out of his "I" and try out a different role, or to look at a situation in life from a different perspective. If we imagine that in this global game there are men and women of different ages and professions, then can I register and become a child, for example, or should I always be myself?

– If I tune into this system, then I have to include everyone around within me. Otherwise I won't be able to connect with them harmoniously. Therefore, I have to experience and understand everyone. That is, I have to reveal all of my qualities and all of the inclinations that exist in me from the beginning, but that are concealed or distorted by Nature for now. I have turned myself into an egoistic mutant! But if I start revealing these qualities inside me, I will discover an ability to feel the whole of Nature—the still, vegetative, and animate parts of it—as well as all of humanity, and even beyond.

When we include everything within us, when all the streams of information, thoughts, and desires pass through me, I begin to feel the following, higher level of Nature, its plan, its overall thought, the cause and effect, its goal, and the final state of my existence.

In every piece or fragment of Nature's actions, we see a cause and effect development with a specific goal at every stage. But we do not see the final goal! Today this final goal is defined as absolute harmony of all parts of Nature.

By uniting among us and with the entire surrounding world, we begin to sense Nature's plan and its final state, the goal. We begin to feel ourselves existing simultaneously at its next level, which is informational, common, and complete.

A person starts to feel eternity, infinity, perfection, that which exists beyond our universe, in the infinite thought of Nature, that which incited this drop of energy to explode and create our universe.

And perhaps we will come to sense or observe our universe conceptually, from aside. But that is already a different mind.

This opens up tremendous perspectives before us. And that is what should happen because the attainment of integrality leads us beyond the boundaries of our universe. It is a breakthrough into the next level of sensation, attainment, and information.

– By entering this global game on the internet and starting to interact there, building the common system, will I be able to imagine this common picture?

– The sensation of integrality, the universal connection on the level of an intelligent human being (homo sapiens) brings you to a state where you include the entire system of Nature within you, including its lower parts—still, vegetative, and animate. That way you start to understand its plan, the inner formula of interconnections.

– When integration becomes your nature, you begin to feel Nature's plan. When you achieve your corrected state, you become a ripe fruit and begin to understand the meaning of your existence. That's when you rise to the next level- Can all this be done through the internet, through a game?

- This is achieved by changing man. And in principle, this is why egoism was given to us. With its help, by constantly ascending above it and changing ourselves in spite of its influence, which seems to halt us and get in our way, we develop ourselves integrally and assimilate into this integration. In other words, egoism constantly helps us to develop.

Similarly, when you're a grade school or college student, you can't advance unless you solve exercises in the process of the study. That is how we develop in Nature, by constantly solving some kind of problem.

There is a very interesting goal before us. Our egoism is like a constantly developing and resurfacing exercise. If we try to solve this exercise, our egoism will transform to connection, mutual love, altruism, and integrality.

Then we will see that we were created this way on purpose. This egoism constantly developed in humanity throughout history, precisely in order to bring us, today, to its intelligent realization in our community. Then, precisely thanks to it, by transcending it, realizing it in what seems like the opposite direction—the direction of connection and integration between us—we will see that it was all created for a purpose, that this is precisely the higher phase of Nature—the egoistic one—and it is pushing us to the next level. What level is that? We will find that out only once we rise. We will simply feel it.

This information, energy, thought, and desire will shift to a completely different level. With their help, by attaining the integral connection between us, we will rise to a different level of existence. I suppose that this will be higher than the initial and final points of our development within the boundaries of this universe. It will be a level above our universe.

REVEALING THE NATURE OF GOODNESS

- Who sets the rules in this integral, global game that can happen over the internet?

- We do. The whole point of the game is that it practically doesn't have any rules. We, the players, gradually create these rules by ourselves. Together, we gradually accept them, approve them, and correct them. We constantly perfect and change them because it is a living system.

We are building an integral community out of ourselves. And in it, you and I determine which laws and rules of behavior we have to observe so we can all spin like cogwheels, function as best as possible, and provide each other with the utmost support.

Let's start developing this system. I am certain that all of this is inherent in Nature. As soon as we start moving according to its plan, which wishes to come to life within us, we will start receiving clues. The crises are happening because we are going against this plan. It's as if we are constantly trying to trip ourselves up.

When we start working according to Nature, we will start having the right thoughts and desires. We will begin to understand each other better, and completely different rules will form. Even our feelings and thoughts will shift from egoistic to integral. We will start solving tasks differently, and we will see completely different layers of Nature, which are more internal. We will see from where Nature governs us.

Today we perceive all of Nature through the lens of our egoism, paying attention only to what is profitable for us or threatens us. I don't see the rest of Nature.

All kinds of things might be happening around me, but I observe the surrounding reality only to the extent of my ego's development—what is good for it and what is bad. I screen all the information and all the influences that affect me through this filter.

It's as if everything else doesn't exist! I don't notice anything else. Suppose that tomorrow my egoism grows bigger (in fact, it is always growing). In that case, I will suddenly discover new phenomena and laws in Nature. Everything is determined by the growth of my egoism.

But if in addition to our growing egoism, we begin to create an integral system among us, then we will let completely different information from Nature pass through to us, into this integral connection. And this information will be altruistic instead of egoistic.

When that happens, we will start to understand Nature's second force—not the egoistic one, which we feel today, and in which we see only a struggle of opposites. Behind this second force, we won't see a struggle, but tremendous kindness, love, and reciprocity, which is exactly what causes life to continue. Life would never have emerged in Nature without the existence of a good force that pushes everything toward unity and growth. Today we seem to observe only the evil force of Nature, but we can discover the good, kind force as well.

Of course, "good force" and "evil force" are just words. Everything is perceived in relation to the observer, but we will discover myriad new things. On the juxtaposition of these two systems—by perceiving Nature egoistically or altruistically—we really would understand the kind of world we live in. Then we could begin to understand our state before birth and after death.

There are a lot of conjectures here, but in general all of this is being revealed to us today as a possible field for research.

– Are you saying that this good force potentially exists, and our task is to reveal it by interacting correctly? I am a bit skeptical. The internet has been in existence for several decades by now.

In Europe and America, an entire generation has already been raised on it who are now 40 years old. As a psychologist, I encounter these people and I know that they have lost the elementary skills of natural physical communication. Therefore, I feel cautious and am wondering whether man will lose these skills if he becomes immersed in our virtual game system?

– Development does not depend on us. In the best case scenario, we are observers, if we are even able to observe and properly assess what is happening, because it depends entirely on the development of our nature.

We have created the internet because our development from within pushed us to do this. We did not create it 100 or 1,000 years ago because our inner, egoistic consciousness and desire did not yet push us to it.

The time has come, so the necessary technological conditions have been created. The need for this kind of communication arose and that's why it emerged and came about. There is no point going back or trying to go against this flow. On the contrary, I would look ahead. After all, through this system humanity is discovering itself as more connected, and not in the physical sense. Besides, what does a connection through our bodies give us?

Today we are not using this connection to the full extent, except to fulfill our petty egoism, to make a profit or manipulate people.

What if we started using the internet as a good, virtual community, which will then elevate us from the virtual connection to the integral, spiritual one? Then, with people's spirit and proper communication, they will acquire a completely different sensation of togetherness and of each other. This is impossible without the internet, so I look at all of this as positive.

In general, I don't see anything negative in humanity or its progress. Of course, this progress could have been much more productive and merciful, but that depends on humanity's behavior in this process, the extent to which we do not resist it, understand it, and participate in it to the best of our ability.

In my opinion, the exit from the physical contact to the virtual, egoistic contact, followed by the transformation of the egoistic, virtual contact to the altruistic, integral one, will bring is to a completely different state. Gradually, we really will lose the sensation of the still, vegetative, and animate world, and will cross over to a state where everything is determined by energy, information, and our thoughts and desires, instead of the comfort of our animate bodies.

This is the next phase of human development. There is no other possibility! This is where Nature is pushing us. The phases we have gone through clearly show that humanity has to climb to the level of thoughts, desires, and information where we are all interconnected. This, strictly speaking, is what defines a community as human. The human community is not our bodies, but precisely the inner filling.

– A few days ago I met a young man who spent all of his time in virtual space. As a result, he lost his job and was evicted from his apartment. The question is: If this virtual space is so attractive and corresponds to the laws of Nature, then where is the correlation between the virtual space and the physical one? Should I still devote time and attention to earning money so I won't be evicted from my apartment?

– This is an important problem: How do we realize ourselves in the integral community in our day-to-day lives? Me, my family, my job, society, and the world—how does our unity on the internet impact our world and our lives, and accordingly, how do we gradually transform our families, our relationships with our relatives and with the people close to us, the government, our country, and the world? How do our social and economic relations change according to this, as well as industry and government? This is an important topic that requires considerable attention.

Today humanity is beginning to feel Nature's challenge—that something unknown and menacing is rising before us. This call of Nature is quickly becoming real, and our problem is only how to partake in this realization in order to feel ourselves swimming along with the flow rather than paddling against it, thus suffering unexpected cataclysms and crises.

- And what if I haphazardly give myself over to this virtual, integral game?

- But you have to participate in it intelligently, understand it, and make independent moves. It requires your live participation. You cannot say, "I'll jump in and let the current take me wherever it goes." The current won't take anyone anywhere because Nature requires that we participate consciously, ascend to a level where we feel the whole world and participate in the process together with everyone. You press on your linkage with the whole world! And this is exactly what Nature requires of us.

Currently, it is leading us on the harsh path, showing us that if we don't press on our linkage with everyone else in order to act congruously, it will hit us. This is the reason for today's crises, which will force us to achieve collaboration.

A Multifaceted
Perception of the World

- Excursions—Getting to Know the World and Choosing the Future
- A Child in Search of Himself
- The Advantage of Higher Education
- Solving the Problem of Drugs
- Total Immersion in Games
- Competition or War?
- A World Soccer Championship
- We Are Evolved Animals
- Infinite Goodness

Some parents prohibit children from playing specific types of games. Is there such a thing as a harmful game, and if so, what is it?

– A game is an imitation of a future state. By imitating adults or independently inventing scenes and situations, a child imagines that he is in those future states. It seems to him that he is actually doing it.

Of course, he doesn't understand why these urges exist in him or how they control him. They are instilled in us by Nature so that we may develop and prepare for future states by acting out the most diverse situations and our behavior in them ahead of time. Whether a game is correct or incorrect, useful or harmful, depends on the kind of child we wish to end up with.

We have to watch very carefully what games a child plays and what children he associates with, what he sees there, what he realizes and understands, and what influences him. Do these games take place in mixed groups of boys and girls, or do boys and girls play separately? Are the children the same age? Are there children from different social circles? Everything must be considered.

If we want to achieve an integral society and we realize that this goal has been placed before us by Nature, and if we know that to achieve it we have to rise above our egoism and establish the right connection among us, we have to check whether all of the child's games lead to that state?

Only the games that teach how to attain this sublime goal can be considered useful.

– The most widespread prohibition applied by parents is on "adventure" games. These are games played individually or in groups, and the player or players must overcome various obstacles to advance from one level to the next. Parents think that this is a harmful game and prohibit playing it. Is it really harmful? And if yes, what is harmful about it?

– I see that children are very attracted to this kind of game. In life they are also constantly crawling, jumping, overcoming something, and climbing on top of something. This is useful for their physical development. If they wish to see the same thing in a virtual game and to try themselves there, I think it is useful.

The whole problem lies in what exactly is the child overcoming? Is he hitting and destroying someone, or does he overcome obstacles together with his peers, learning about integration with others in the process?

I don't think we should entirely take away this kind of interaction and the need to overcome difficulties. On the contrary, let them get confused and look for a way out, because this is natural for a person. Our entire life is a search for the best possibility out of several, and a continuous process of overcoming obstacles.

Let's not turn a child into a passive observer. It's very useful to interact with what is happening, so this kind of game is necessary. The whole problem is the meaning of these games, their content, where they lead a child, and what a child gets out of the game in the end.

EXCURSIONS—GETTING TO KNOW THE WORLD AND CHOOSING THE FUTURE

Children go out on excursions to the real world where they visit factories and other establishments. Should a child retain a sensation that this is a game, or should he participate in reality seriously, starting with childhood?

– Of course, he has to see real life. Excursions facilitate a multifaceted perception of the world. A child sees what adults are occupied with and imagines how in the future he will also take part in productive, mental, moral, physical, and social processes by participating in them.

A child should be placed in situations that will pose questions before him: Does this suit me or not? How would I act in this case? Do I like this profession or not? What is special about it? What is its purpose and what benefit does it bring to society and to myself? Does it contradict what we are talking about? We have to discuss all of this.

In this regard it is necessary to keep track not just of a child's reaction, but also the phases of his maturation, as well as how he sees himself in this process. How much does he research the actual production and its importance for humanity, and accordingly, does he decide that "I choose this activity because people need this work," or "I choose it because it's interesting to me"?

Excursions have to be discussed from all sides. I would say that they aren't just excursions, but the attainment of the world, which gives a child the opportunity to see himself in the future, and to ask the question, "Who will I be when I grow up?" Children have to imagine themselves in each role they have seen. This is very important because any place they visit provides an enormous collection of feelings and sensations which are so vital for a child.

There are children who carry a mouse or a frog in their pocket, while others cannot stand to look at these creatures. Some are drawn to technology or music, while others can work physically from dawn to dusk, and others still are able only to think while sitting down. After all, we understand how diverse people are.

Every child has to try out everything in order to form himself and to find his own place in life. Excursions provide a constant and maximally wide familiarity with all forms of human activity.

A CHILD IN SEARCH OF HIMSELF

– One of the most important characteristics of a game is its competitive aspect.

There is a book titled *How to Become the Parent You Never Had: A Treatment for Extremes of Fear, Anger and Guilt*. This book starts out by saying that we are all winners because 500 million sperm cells competed, and the winner was...

– Me.

– Yes, I won. Since this competitive element was enrooted in us by Nature itself, how can we use it correctly?

– Let's not talk about chance or about how this is programmed in Nature. In this particular competition the winner is the strongest one, the one who has special qualities.

A person who participates in the life of society or the environment on a multifaceted plane might be better than others in one way and worse than others in another way. But if every person finds the best way to apply his fortes and abilities, then the flaws of one person are "covered" by the merits of another. A happy person is one who has found the optimal way to fulfill himself, and this is something he has to discern within. If he can be fast, alert, and steadfast, if he can overcome adversity and win over others, then his victory will benefit him and the people around him.

I would particularly like to underline that the victory will be virtuous if its aim is to use one's abilities to provide maximal help to the environment, to society. Then it will be expressed in the common human system and will remain impressed there, and will be recorded in his account.

But if a person realizes himself incorrectly, then despite having wonderful talents, he will have the opposite result. We have to bring every child's abilities to light and encourage their development.

When I was starting out in college, it was very fashionable to major in science and technical fields, and these departments tried to lure everyone in. I remember how agitated the students were and how great the disappointment was afterwards.

I understand and respectfully recall several of my classmates who left the studies not because they weren't successful. They saw that technical studies did not have the romance they had dreamed of. Working with impulses and calculating parameters? They became convinced that this was absolutely not the profession they wanted. They left without much hesitation, and they were right to do so because they found their calling elsewhere.

In our system of upbringing we are trying to recognize a child's inclinations early on so he won't make mistakes. He has to see and become familiar with all the areas of human activity, and find himself during the period of his upbringing in our system. The search for the appropriate profession is very important and takes up a lot of time in our life. It's a joy when a person finds himself in a certain profession.

– So there is nothing dangerous about expressing special talents, and we shouldn't try to even children out?

– No. On the contrary, we have to bring out their talents during the teenage period. We are preparing children so that by age 13 or 14 they will start studying a university level curriculum.

Before that they have to clearly discern what is right for them. Our task is to push them to make the choice that fits their inclinations instead of being dependent on opportunities to rise on the corporate ladder or the size of their future salary.

– But is their contribution to the common good always evaluated?

– Of course. Otherwise one's inner parameters will not correspond to the chosen profession, he won't benefit anyone, and he won't be happy with himself either. The right solution to this problem is good both for the individual and the society.

I remember how back in my time everyone across the board entered technical departments because this was in high demand by the government and the times required it. Everyone else were looked down on. Pedagogical and humanitarian departments became empty since everyone went into science and engineering.

As a result, I think the true value of this generation was never revealed. It quickly became exhausted, leaving behind a hollow-hearted environmen- Yes, there is even a term, "the technical intelligentsia," which was in many ways not occupied by technical matters, but the liberal arts.

– When I wrote my dissertation at Russia's Institute of Philosophy, I found many former "techies" there. But once people received a technical education, they left and learned some other profession because in their youth they were lured to the wrong place, so later they still changed their profession.

THE ADVANTAGE OF HIGHER EDUCATION

– You have repeatedly spoken about how important it is for a child to receive a higher education as early as the teenage years. Why is this important, and why should a teenager spend so much time on this?

– I think it is necessary. Besides, the modern school can only harm a person.

Higher education trains a person to work with books, visit libraries, participate in laboratory work, and take exams. It keeps him in motion. He has to participate in these processes, understand how to study different subjects, how to choose textbooks and study them, how to choose the necessary material and report on it, and how to carry out lab work. This gives him the skills to be self-sufficient in life.

In school, children simply come to class, sit there, everything is chewed up for them, they nod their heads, get grades, and go home. Today's schools kill all independence. When a child finishes school, he is incapable of active achievement and self-study. But a college provides him with that, at least partially.

By slightly altering school and college, we will have a person who can develop independently for the rest of his life. Today, people who finish school or college do not receive the necessary skills to progress through life independently. They remain simple performers.

– In schools and universities, there is a notion of a "nerd." This is a person who scrupulously carries out all the assignments and does everything "by the book." On the opposite side of the "nerd" are shrewd young men and women who cut corners and find unconventional, new moves, and thus reach the goal by the short path. From your point of view, which path is better and more preferable for raising a child?

– These are completely different types of people. We have to give everyone the opportunity to start their own research in laboratories in different departments from the youngest age.

When I was growing up, there was a youth center close to our house. There were many laboratories in that house, like photography, physics, botany, and zoology. Back then, all of these things were innovations. Besides this, there were plenty of athletic clubs.

In my opinion, as part of the study process it is necessary to set aside time for additional scientific work so the students can try themselves out.

What remains in a person's memory after college is precisely the lab projects where he did something on his own in practice, where he came up with results, calculated them, and so on. Everything else leaves very dim recollections of bogus formulas that are disconnected from real work.

"Nerds" and those who "tear the stars down from the sky" have different approaches to life. Both need to be given an opportunity to develop.

I don't see any other way besides letting each student work independently. But we definitely have to ask him: What do you do besides the study program? Do you participate in anything? Where are your scientific achievements? The degree of their scientific character is not important. What's important is that this forces a person to look for the necessary material in libraries and in scientific periodicals, and gives him an opportunity to create.

– Who should work as instructors, teachers, and educators in these shops and laboratories?

– The college staff.

It is very good to engage in scientific activity during college. I think it is also necessary to lessen the students' load, to free them up from excessive theoretical subjects, and give them a chance to participate in scientific research.

– From what age does it make sense to organize these "scientific" clubs for children?

– I felt a calling to go into engineering and wanted to study it from age 9 or 10. I clearly remember that in our small city I did not find anything besides the youth center with its hobby clubs.

It is during childhood that a child begins to take interest in something specific. On our part, we have to support him in every way we can.

Right now we are mainly talking about upbringing. But upbringing has to happen together with education. How? Education works together with upbringing to the extent that one's education is useful for the world. Only in the case of usefulness will education be not only in demand by others, but it will also bring about success, and alongside that, the child will be able to advance. His useful activity for others will be affirmed in Nature because it will be supported by Nature.

A person must know exactly to what extent his hobby or interest is necessary, if it fits into the common flow, and if it is connected to the main directions of society's development. If not, then all of his work will be unsustainable.

SOLVING THE PROBLEM OF DRUGS

- I would like to touch on the topic of drugs. This is also a kind of game in a sense because through drugs a person enters a new state and changes. So what's so bad about drugs?

- The fact that a person becomes detached from reality, nothing else is bad about it. A person becomes detached from society and from life. He doesn't do anything bad to anyone, and he is peacefully walking down the street with a glassy gaze, not seeing anyone. He cannot be considered a socially harmful element, but he causes harm by going against Nature, and we do not agree with this.

In general, drugs are very cheap. It's possible to constantly feed them to 3 or 4 billion of the "extra" people on earth so that the rest can live in peace. We can shut them off from all the problems that way. We could hand out drugs to the masses and the crime rate would immediately drop. We could house them on reservations and let them sit there peacefully, getting high and having a ball.

However, the fact is that we inherently oppose this kind of attitude to life. Humanity cannot agree to this despite the fact that these actions are harmless to society and even useful in a sense. Nature has prescribed the goal of our existence so powerfully within us that we cannot passively observe a person who voluntarily detaches himself from a sober, adult life.

Therefore, we don't agree to it. We don't want to take this opportunity to be in nirvana for the rest of our lives and then to peacefully die. On the surface it might seem that nothing could be better. After all, life is full of disappointments, searches, troubles, and depression. But still, we don't agree to this.

And we can defeat this evil by giving a person satisfaction with what he does, the sensation of a fulfilled life. Then he won't need to cut himself off from life. But if his entire life consists of endless suffering and emptiness, then we cannot blame him for opting for drugs.

I read a speech by the chief of Russia's health ministry where he says that in the next decade, up to half of the country's population will be depressed, and today the rate is already 25%. And this is a declaration by the chief of the health ministry; these are the numbers he makes public! And how many more people are there who are not counted? What can be done with such a mass?

It is the same situation throughout the world. There are countries with even higher rates. Divorce, violence on a massive scale, terrorism—it is all part of the common problem of enormous inner emptiness. And it has to be filled by something. Otherwise...

We shouldn't be fighting the drugs, but rather the reason that makes people want them. And that reason is the emptiness within us, which can only be filled by what Nature has prepared for us.

Why does the sensation of emptiness arise? And what can it be filled with? In our time we have to rise to the level of integral unification with everyone, and fill ourselves with that. That is how we will come to feel the common nature, its eternity and perfection, and will become included in it, identify ourselves with it. We will flow in that eternity.

We will still live the life on earth—where we will realize our integration with others—while sensing ourselves on an order above this world, on the level of a human being rather than an animal or a partially successful social element.

By making a person part of the global, integral society, we will tear him away from drugs and he won't need them anymore.

He will experience states of attainment, the search for perfection, and he will acquire harmony that is thousands of times more powerful than when he is under the influence of any chemical substance.

TOTAL IMMERSION IN GAMES

– There is one more type of game that has captivated hundreds of millions of people: gambling games, such as casinos and cards. Their popularity is constantly growing. Why? And what is dangerous about these games? In your school of integral, global upbringing, is there a place for venturesome games? And if not, why?

– Competition is a good thing. It doesn't matter with what or with whom you are competing—a roulette wheel, a slot machine, or other people. In any case, you enter a contest. That is, you wish to rise above a certain circumstance, phenomenon, or incident. You want to ascend and affirm yourself.

It's very interesting to observe people who play. I spent an entire week in Las Vegas observing my wife, who went crazy over the games. At home she is a regular, normal grandmother. But when she found herself among the "one armed bandits," she lost her head.

When a grown up woman with two university degrees, living at the other end of the world, very far away from Las Vegas, finds herself in this place, something unclear ignites in her, some strange force draws her to the risky game.

Together we decided that we could spend $50 an evening to play a game that costs 10 or 20 cents a shot. She played and I observed from the side, watching the human being in her disappear and turn into the same "one armed bandit." A machine ends up playing with a machine, they compete, and there's nothing more than that.

I use my wife as an example because she is a normal, level-headed woman, without any particular vices, very grounded and balanced. It's simply astounding what takes place inside of us. A person has a need to rise above chance, above himself, above this machine, meaning to affirm himself.

And if we give a person the opportunity to compete for something that is good and useful for society, then he will be able to satisfy this necessity. It exists and it cannot be suppressed. Therefore, it's necessary to give a person the opportunity to reflect, create, participate, win, and affirm himself. This is possible in the integral society because there, every one of us is a distinct individual.

At the same time, every one of us is just a cogwheel that is very small and has nothing special about it. But sometimes it starts to slow down or changes direction, causing itself to stand out from the others. By spinning harmoniously with everyone, it expresses itself to the utmost, and at the same time experiences fulfillment and satisfaction.

Integral upbringing will give a person the opportunity to find himself in the game called life. We will feel that we are constantly moving forward, and that like children, we are acting out and realizing a higher state, and behind it a new, higher state emerges. This enthralling adventure, a never-ending ascent, will be felt by every person.

People are looking for drugs and gambling games, ready to jump off a bridge into an abyss in search of intense sensations. A person will find all of this in the integral interaction with others because it holds astounding opportunities for self-realization. Then, today's extremes won't be something that really fulfills people.

– If I understand you correctly, we will be able to realize the quality of risk-taking precisely through the constant change of states?

– Nature has built us in a way that the only way for us to fully and harmoniously realize ourselves is in integration. Then we won't have to "let out steam" by getting drunk, getting into fights, or throwing stadium frenzies because there won't be any unrealized necessities left. We have to see the real field of our activity in the integral connection. This is the field we were created for, the venue where we reveal and correct our innermost, darkest instincts.

COMPETITION OR WAR?

If a person perceived the world as an integral whole, he would see that all of his urges are realized in the form of correct contacts with others, positive and negative alike. Then he would no longer have to harbor any pent-up feelings, having to restrain himself.

Take soccer for example. If this game is realized correctly, if the teams are permeated by friendship, then the game can be filled with love. It will be a competition of friends who receive satisfaction from the actual process of the game.

In this game, one person's superiority over another will lie in the answer to the questions: What was your inner experience? What was the goal for which we played? How did we collate ourselves with others? How were our positive or negative qualities expressed?

You can experience the most astonishing states here: you play a game with your egoism and against it, establish contact with your friends and with the opponent, suppressing the aspiration to stand out or, vice versa, expressing yourself and standing out, but for the sake of the team. Today none of this exists in soccer; it's become a business.

This moral, inner, spiritual research of oneself and others during this externally harsh game holds enormous opportunities for "intellectual" soccer players.

I think that any competition—besides those where we inflict harm on others, such as hunting—is a venue where we can discern a person's attitude toward others and express it in bold relief. The elements of the game will enable one to develop and attain a state of enormous self-attainment.

– Should we change the rules of the game, or discuss and analyze what happened and how it happened after the game? Should we watch video recordings of the game and go over the situations that occurred during the game?

– I think the game should be stopped every ten minutes in order to do a "restart" and return all the players to the correct state. They should check: What did we attain over these 10 minutes? What kind of inner work did each person succeed in performing? How did he look at others? How did he receive a pass? How did he steal the ball? How did he participate in connecting with others? And how did he treat his opponent?

Ten minutes of inner work is a lot. The ball, the field, and the game are just external excuses to conduct an inner self-analysis.

Today we can't even imagine how to conduct a true evaluation of our inner realization, which is the work of the winners. But I think we will get there and we will learn to take energy expenditures and intentions into account. This will allow us to weigh teams of players as a whole and each player in particular.

– What is the right mindset in a game?

– The right mindset is one that's aimed at unity and integrality. In Nature, there are two seemingly opposite forces—a positive one and a negative one. The opposition in a game depends on how we combine our individual, egoistic vectors within a team.

When we unite in a team, what do we play with the opponents? In other words: What is the victory? It's very important to discern this. A goal someone has scored is not a victory. On the level of our world it is a physical achievement. But above it, internally, we played a game of unification, the game of suppressing ourselves and connecting on a higher level, above ourselves.

What was the result that we reached through this inner game, the passes of our own egoistic and altruistic forces and qualities? Which points did each of us count for himself? How much did he advance in his self-analysis during this game?

These games have tremendous potential to help us go through levels of internal development quickly. This is a question of the future, but I don't think it is too far off.

Any forms of human activity, especially forms that include competitive elements on the level of our world, can give us an enormous opportunity to build opposite actions above them and to analyze.

THE WORLD SOCCER CHAMPIONSHIP

- As children we used to play "suicide checkers" and other "anti-games." For example, in soccer the goal was not to win, but to give in and lose. Are you now talking about this kind of anti-game?

- No! On the level of our world we have to play by strictly observing all the rules. And each of us plays by realizing the opportunities given to him, without giving in to anyone.

But above this mechanical competition, how do we elevate our intention, build unity, and the right attitude to one another? How do we compete with one another? It's done in the intention, and not just the physical competition.

The game remains the same, but becomes more correct and conducted by the rules. It is played without any particularly harsh offenses, in a very "gentlemanly" manner, but no more than that.

Above this we build relationships within every team and between the teams so that the system composed of 22 players on a green field would appear absolutely harmonious to the spectators, consisting of elements that are opposite yet interconnected by a harmonious and conscious connection.

This meaning has to be realized in all forms of human activity. This world remains the same material world, consisting of many qualities and controlled by two opposite forces, which we have to unite. Man is a being that connects all the opposing forces of Nature in order to attain a single goal, harmony.

– Say there is a world soccer championship, and it has reached the final. Two billion people are watching this event. There are two teams that realize their mastery to the maximum. The game is progressing beautifully, in grand style. And you're saying that it doesn't matter who wins? Then what's the outcome of it?

– All the players and spectators achieve profound unity. This is the goal of the process called "soccer."

– And this is not happening at the current world championship?

– What are you talking about!? At the current world championship one player is paid 10 million dollars, another is paid 5 million, and another receives 2 million, and they all play just for this. They don't even care what team they play for. They'll go wherever they are paid most.

Give me a billion dollars and I will gather up a team that will tear apart the whole world. It's only a matter of money and nothing else. But if the inequality of the teams becomes obvious, then people will lose interest in the game and there will be nothing to make them watch. Soccer is a business, so there is a consensus among the competitors to gather up teams that are more or less equal in order to lure spectators into the arena.

This is a sheer lie, a show. The games themselves are fixed and how they will proceed is known even before the game starts. Two billion people get worked up because someone agitates them, someone processes them intentionally, winding them up with "bread and games."

And most importantly, what is the result? A mass beating of the fans.

– Usually, yes.

– There's the celebration of friendship and sports for you.

WE ARE EVOLVED ANIMALS

– How can a soccer match be built so there is a feeling of unity afterwards?

– Friendship is seriously missing in today's sports. Many people talk about friendship, but competition is an expression of egoism. I am egoistically trying to achieve the maximum result, but by the rules.

If only we would see the inner, moral, and spiritual tension of a person who wishes to compete in order to attain a connection with others! I can reach this state by competing with you at throwing a javelin, for example. It is precisely competition in this world that gives a person the kind of connection with other people, that allows him to rise above to create a place of mutual unification.

– The result is mutu– It's mutual in every way! It affects the entire system of human relations. On the inside we will remain individualists and egoists who hate each other, and this feeling will be expressed in us more and more strongly, but above it we will have to discern our common superstructure of love. When these two levels become expressed in their full might, they will give us the sensation of the entire depth of the eternal, perfect nature, making us equal to it.

Can you imagine how these great achievements will change man? On the one hand, there is hatred, repulsion, and separation from others; and in sports the aspiration is to win no matter what. On the other hand, there is love, at the same time, total dependence and friendship, as if you are competing with your beloved child.

You would happily lose to him on purpose. But here you don't do that. Here you have to act on both of these levels without pretending; you have to do it for real. As a psychologist, can you imagine such discernments?

– No, it's pretty hard for me to imagine it.

– What a psychologically complex concept! One has to come out of oneself, this is what has to happen in a person. That is how he will enter the next level, ascend into a different system, a different dimension.

There are three levels in Nature: still, vegetative, and animate. We are evolved animals. But when we unite on this level and begin to rise above ourselves, we enter the "human" level, which we didn't know before. This is the level of common harmony.

– The enormous potential of this action is clear. I just don't understand how this unification is supposed to happen. How can we do it?

– Through gradual upbringing. There is no other way. This is the challenge that Nature has placed before us. This is exactly why we are entering the inclusive crisis today. It has to teach us how to rise above ourselves while maintaining today's level in everything.

Everything that is currently done on earth will remain. We don't have to break anything. Of course, we will eliminate the harmful production. But our task is to raise ourselves above this world, above the physical actions through self-education, self-attainment, and the right upbringing.

– One of the definitions of love is to receive pleasure from whatever gives the other person pleasure...

– In spite of my hatred for him! This hatred is not eliminated. Otherwise the tension would be removed from the love and you would have to quarrel to feel the love more intensely.

– In this team of 22 players, during the break after 10 minutes of playing I have to think about how much pleasure my friend from the other team experienced?

– Not only that. You have to aspire to unite on the level of opposite physical actions and goals, as well as on the level of the inner actions and the goal.

– In thought?

– Yes, in thought. This is exactly inner, creative activity by which man creates himself and raises himself above the physical world.

INFINITE GOODNESS

– Is our task as educators to use people's egoistic potential to gradually build the system of interaction above it?

– This is exactly how that potential is actualized. It cannot be realized any other way because it is suppressed by everyone else. We are always limited, as if we are in jail with our hands tied.

To the extent we can unite with each other, rising above our egoism, we will see that we can let it go, shake free of its shackles. To the extent that we prepare an intention to connect ahead of time, we can be free from egoism. Then we will see how everything is immediately realized wonderfully, how we are truly free and don't have to limit ourselves.

There is nowhere to hide from egoism. And we don't have to! It's growing, and that's great! You only have to build your connection with others above it, and then this egoism will exist for a good cause.

– This is really inspiring, on the conceptual level. But in the practical sense, what does a child need in order to take this step toward other people?

– He must be in daily contact with the rest of the children under the educator's supervision.

– What has to happen there? Does he have to see another person?

– A child starts to perceive reality even before he is born. But we are talking about children at an age when they can be accepted into a group and certain physical boundaries and limits can be introduced.

A two-year-old child expresses very rudimentary needs for a collective, such as for someone he can play with or look at. Before that, he barely notices others.

From this age on, we accept children into this system, which helps them develop the right sensation of others, a sensation of the "neighbor" and the right attitude toward him. If a child is brought up this way, there is no doubt that within a few years he will become an integral element of society.

Egoism surfaces in him and is simultaneously compensated. It's not an attempt to level it, but precisely its supplementation with altruistic intentions. A child develops harmoniously, without feeling any limitations whatsoever from his parents, school, and educators.

By receiving the correct upbringing, he easily and freely adapts egoism to any circumstances and discovers that Nature brings him only goodness, that all the "negative" qualities are there to warn him, "That's not allowed! Don't touch this! Don't do that! This is not yours!"

When a person builds the right intention over the egoism, he discovers that nothing is forbidden, that Nature is infinitely good in everything it does to him and in the way it leads us.

– What is the right intention?

– Integrality, the right interconnection. When I include another person's desires into my own, and he does the same, then we are treating each other the right way.

We are both egoists, but above our egoism we build a reciprocal interface so that I perceive his egoism as mine and he perceives my egoism as his. It turns out that we are both working on our common egoism. That is, we spin simultaneously like two wheels, without any resistance to one another.

Suppose he has 50 pounds of egoism and I have 100. His egoism is against me and mine is against him. But if above this egoism we build our mutual action and become included in one another, then we begin to perceive the system that raises us above the level of our interlinked egoism; we feel integration, love, and connection. Our mutual attainment corresponds to the common egoism that we use to connect with one another.

Our intentions can be measured in units of our inner efforts. Of course, this is difficult to do today. We still cannot measure a person's ethical and moral efforts. But in principle, this can be measured.

We are building a new layer of a person's existence, a new dimension. Let's call it "spiritual." This is the future of humanity where everything that is on the earthly level will become the foundation for the superstructure that we have to create.

When egoism grows to its maximum level and we fully realize it, we will relocate to that superstructure with our thoughts and feelings and will stop feeling our existence on the earthly level completely. It will simply disappear from our sensations. My "I" will exist only in the spiritual superstructure, and I will associate myself only with this layer.

Integral Perception of Information

- A Person and the Environment
- The Superior Quality of the Collective
- Not a Crowd, but a Sense of Unity
- Individualistic Sensations Are Flawed
- The World Is a Juxtaposition of Opposites
- Everything Is Within Us, There Is Nothing Outside
- The World as a Mirror of Our Imperfection
- Me and Others Become "WE"
- Punishment Is Unnecessary in the Right Society
- Curing Mass Depression
- The Model of Sanctity
- An Anecdote Is a Paradoxical Expression of Integration

– When we talk about perception of reality, I don't really understand what you mean and there are many questions left.

– Give me a summary of what you know about the perception of reality from the standpoint of psychology, and I will tell you what I know from the standpoint of my profession.

– This is an entire field in general psychology and over the last century, great discoveries have been made in it, especially during combat in the Second World War and its aftermath. As strange as it may seem, this was precisely the time when great discoveries such as Kurt Lewin's theory were made. Lewin's theory is about the psychological force field. Lewin was no less of a genius than Freud, but most people ignore his theory and continue to live as they always have.

The discovery he made is that a person's perception is determined by his necessity, that it is not closed off within the person, but that perception is a system that consists of both a person and the environment. Accordingly, the necessity of the pressure is formed precisely in an environment, which changes a person's perception of the external world.

We've said that when children unite in a group the right way, something emerges that enables a child to perceive fundamentally new information, which he could never discover on his own. What is that information, what is so special about this force field, and how does this mechanism work?

– Are you talking about the possibility of integral perception of information?

– Yes.

A PERSON AND THE ENVIRONMENT

– In fact, there is individual and integral perception. Individual perception is also integral, but unconsciously. There is also integral information that is perceived consciously, which enables one to attune and expand the boundaries of perception. As a perceiving object, I can attune and form myself under the influence of a surrounding environment that I chose in advance, by encountering and coming in contact with it, thus entering an integral connection with it.

This happens in life as well. If I want to be a computer programmer, I have to go to a programming workshop that is staffed by good programmers. I have to listen to them praising their mastery, caring for it, and admiring good workmanship. That way they will evoke my desire or aspiration to this profession. Then I will be able to expand the boundaries of my perception, I will acquire specific sensations and a sensitivity for things that I completely didn't feel before.

Everything depends on the environment. If you leave a baby in the forest, it will grow up an animal. Depending on the environment you place it in, that is what it will become. This points to the fact that a person can be formed and regulated.

It's not that he will become different. We have already noticed a while ago that we are a product of the environment. But how to change ourselves under the influence of the environment is, of course, a very interesting question. We look ahead, research it, and form groups of children to elucidate it.

We are looking for possibilities to unite children by shared qualities, specific abilities, or a natural inclination toward something specific. Or vice versa, we can create groups out of completely opposite individuals who will unite with each other to create a diverse collective. The research can be very interesting.

THE SUPERIOR QUALITY OF THE COLLECTIVE

– When the right unification occurs and the children create a unified space, does new information become revealed automatically? Is it already present in this field or does it have to be conveyed with the help of people who are more prepared, the educators?

– The collective has a special quality: When separate people unite into "one whole," they reveal the unity of their opposites.

This holds within it a completely new quality, since none of the individuals have unity within them. This new quality is formed among them, or above them, and each member of the collective participates in creating it. If a person doesn't make efforts and doesn't give of himself to this unity, then he doesn't exist in it.

It turns out that every person tunes into this unity and acquires it to the fullest extent without it splitting into parts. And thanks to one's contribution to this common field, common desire or aspiration, through the integration each person begins to sense unity and a new level of perception.

Perception through integration is completely opposite to the egoistic, individual perception. A person who has it feels and perceives the world in a slightly different way.

As he becomes included in others, it's as if he consists of them. He feels them within him and experiences the common unity. He also feels the world within him, and the perception of the world depends on his qualities, inclinations, state, mood, attitude toward the world, and toward himself. That is, he suddenly starts to understand that the world doesn't exist on the outside, but within him.

This happens completely naturally, a result of the uniting his friends' opposite qualities within him. Together, they form one common desire that becomes the platform upon which he feels a new, integral world, while at the same time becoming an integral vessel himself, an organ of perception.

A person already understands that the world does not exist externally. But when he begins to see the world's total dependence on him, a psychological shift occurs in him.

However, the world depended on him even before that. It's just that he was immersed in his individualism and could not perceive reality as anything but existing outside of him. Yet, this was a false picture of the world.

Now, having come out of individualism into the integral perception of the world, he understands that everything was that way before as well, and that perception occurs only in this way. We perceive the world inside of us, in our qualities. Under the influence of society or the environment, we gain the abilities to change these qualities, to somehow alter them. Now a person does not see the world only through the quality that seems to him as his own, but also through all the other, external qualities, which he now perceives as his own.

If we take a child—as opposed to an adult who has a load of impressions and perceptions from his previous life—and completely isolate him, the child will feel the world within him. Everything depends on which impressions a person receives during his life.

NOT A CROWD, BUT A SENSE OF UNITY

- How many people should there be in a group? Psychologists have noticed that a group of 8-12 people is optimal because it simulates a model of society.

- That is exactly what we do: We have a group of 10 children plus 2 educators.

- In this group of 10 children and 2 educators, a new quality and a new perception emerge. If we gathered a thousand or 10 thousand people, would it be even more vivid?

- The amount of people is less significance. What's most important is whether or not they can unite with each other, and that depends on a person's ability to transcend the ego for the sake of uniting with the society, on his sensitivity, on how developed his sense of the collective is.

Unification under the influence of a crowd does not produce any results. It is not an integral interaction. A crowd united by a common slogan, tearing at some animate goal, is not an integral society.

For people to unite into an integral society, they must be doing it to find the quality of mutual bestowal, unification, unity. In this case each of them rises above his egoism and unites with others in spite of his "crass" natural drives. He is not driven by the desire for personal fulfillment because it will never let him unite with others.

This unity is their newly acquired organ of perception that does not operate inside, but outside. That is how it's aimed—from within outwards, toward bestowal. It can be created only by rising above the ego when each transcends oneself toward bonding with others, above one's egoism. And therefore, this feeling cannot be private but only common.

It's common because it exists through the fact that we create it together, and each of us perceives it as his own sense of external, altruistic perception. It is one for all of us, meaning that it is one and the same inside each of us.

This gives us the opportunity to speak about our common heart and mind, which we produced together and inside of which we exist together. In that case we perceive everything absolutely identically, with the same thoughts and feelings circulating inside of us.

We ascend to a level of feeling the world existing outside of us. In reality, this world is inside of us, but we start to feel it by coming out of the previous egoistic state, and we feel it all together. Meaning, as we develop each new level, we will attain it together.

We perceive each new level as existence that does not depend on each of us individually. This means that it does not depend on our bodies or on our current "I." If I sympathize with "I" that exists in this integration, then I detach from my earthly life.

This life seems increasingly hazier and less real to me. I begin to understand that my body and all of my previous impressions and sensations of the world and of life took place in the egoistic perception. But now I cross over to a new state and see the world differently.

The integral perception of the world gives me new, more vivid impressions. The past becomes gradually more distant and less important, uninteresting, very flat and childish. I am so unimpressed by it that I am ready to part with it without regretting it in the least.

A person develops his new, integral state to such an extent that the past disappears.

We think, "How can it disappear!? After all, here are our bodies!" We don't understand that these bodies exist only in our perception, which constantly changes. That's how we change the sensation of our world to the sensation of the world that is on the next level. But there it also exists in our common desire and thought, while the bodies, as such, do not exist. Only thoughts and desires do.

INDIVIDUALISTIC SENSATIONS ARE FLAWED

– Suppose there is a group of people who are united by a common desire to attain this lofty goal. What happens when a new person appears in this group? Do we have to include him into this system? How does that happen?

– To the extent he adapts to the group, he'll find himself in the new, integral sense of perception, in a world that's higher than the earthly one.

He feels the earth with his individual perception. But he can exist in the spiritual world if he has aspirations that are shared with the group that forms this integral sense.

– This means that the material level gradually becomes unimportant, like a background. But does it remain in one's perception?

– It remains in one's perception because we exist in a society that exists in the individual perception of the world, as opposed to its integral perception. As long as there is such a great number of individualists, we are surrounded by their perception of the world. They project their incorrect, individualistic sensations on us because we are a single whole and are all integrally interconnected.

The picture of the mutual universal dependence is starting to be revealed in our world only now, but in fact, we were always that way. I hope that this revelation will happen in the near future, if not in our generation, then in the next, or the one after it. Judging by the speed of the movement towards the expression of this integration, we can suppose that it will become clear very soon.

The whole world has to reach the understanding that the desirable state is the correct perception of reality, meaning one that isn't distorted as in this world, where we exist in a small fragment of the entire universe. Everyone will reach this understanding, voluntarily or involuntarily.

In this world, we exist in an uncertain state where our perception is fragmentary and very hazy. There are certain vague, internal foretastes: something exists, existed, and will exist. There are riddles and answers. Fortunetellers' forecasts come true, and everyone says there is destiny and life after death.

We have to understand that the true state will be revealed when we become similar to the integral nature, when we become the same single whole as Nature and connect all of Nature's other parts through ourselves.

Then we will discover that all of its parts were always connected. It was only in man's egoism that he perceived everything as divided, thus ruining everything inside of him. But outside of us, Nature is absolutely ideal, seamless, and perfect. By revealing this, we become the same as it, thus rising to its level of perfection and eternity.

THE WORLD IS A JUXTAPOSITION OF OPPOSITES

– A friend of mine who works as a tour guide in India started having difficulties at work because the tourists say she is in nirvana, does not react adequately, and cannot explain anything properly. Won't the children entering this integral system become like angels, detached from reality?

– No. I would not call this state angelic. The schizophrenic, painful, and incorrect division of the world into parts is explained by the fact that a person does not correct himself.

He is not working with his egoism to rise above it and perceive two levels of attitude to life. He is not prepared for this and is not in a collective that can create a new sense together with him.

Your friend is an unfortunate woman who is risking losing her normal, egoistic, earthly approach to life and ending up in a bad, inadequate state. Our upbringing is not based on the Indian method, which destroys or reduces egoism, but on developing it, as strange as it may sound. We are saying that everything is built upon the juxtaposition of opposites.

The world is not a struggle of opposites, but rather their proper combination. Dialectics is right in saying that the world consists of two opposites, but it is mistaken in thinking that one of them should be destroyed.

One of them should be raised above the other and the two of them should be used correctly, like dumbbells. This is a dipole. Within the tension between the plus and the minus, we can find the quality that connects them. With its help we will discover the true, integral world. It is integral; it does not destroy any of its parts.

I understand this woman's state, but I cannot offer her any counsel. This does not happen to our children. On the contrary, every day a healthy egoism is expressed in them even more, and they become coarser, tougher. However, they understand where their egoism comes from.

At the same time, we conduct practical and theoretical studies with them in order to make this egoism clearer, understand it, separate from it, and research it from aside, studying both one's own egoism and that of others. Everyone changes places in order to become included in one another: Right now I am like you, you are like him, and so on.

I have to know all my friends, come out of myself, and play the role of each of them. This enables us to become integrally included in one another, and this mutual inclusion gradually creates a new entity—integral perception, which does not include "me" but only "we."

EVERYTHING IS WITHIN US, THERE IS NOTHING OUTSIDE

– Why did people suddenly start uniting? They could have done that 100 or 200 years ago, to unite and reveal spirituality. But for some reason that didn't happen. Moreover, people only started talking about group interaction in the 20th century. Forming groups and discussing common questions is an innovation of the 20th century. In the past this kind of thing simply didn't exist.

– Science has existed since ancient times. For example, Aristotle, Plato, and their predecessors wrote about the soul, about perception, and looked for the place where the soul exists. Yet, psychology as a science emerged and developed only in the 20th century.

Why did people wait so many centuries!? Where were these scientists a few thousand years ago, throughout which man did not understand who he is and what he is? There were some attempts to study ourselves before as well, but they were done on such a primitive level that one could only feel ashamed for those people!

They built cities, countries, conquered lands, and ruled them, but they couldn't know anything about themselves. They discovered new lands, developed technologies and economy, and made revolutions. But what drove them to do that? Why didn't they have an inner demand or need to find out, "Man, who are you?"

Apparently, this depends on our inner development. This necessity did not arise in us before, and therefore we did not engage in it; we didn't have this question. If there is no question, then there is nothing to reveal and nothing to work on. I don't have a 6th finger on my hand, and I don't feel a need for it. So how can I wish for it to grow on my hand?

We are now entering a specific phase of development where an inner demand to know ourselves is being revealed in us. It is emerging because we have to enter the next level of perception and attainment.

Modern psychology formed 100 years ago and continues to develop to this day. But look at how it's become part of our lives. Previously, it wasn't a fashionable hobby even for the aristocrats, not to mention housewives. They couldn't care less about psychology.

But now the world is becoming integral, interconnected, and interdependent. And the need is emerging to become familiar with psychology—that of the masses, the crowd, the individual, different nations, people of different ages, and the psychology of the family.

We are increasingly connecting a person's inner state to his perception and attainment of the world, to his worldview. We are starting to feel that the world is a result or function of our inner states.

Parallel to psychology, the same ideas are being developed in physics. Einstein thought that everything in the world is relative, and Hugh Everett thought the same. Yet physics seems like a dry science. We think, "Oh well, engineering, what's the big deal, really?" But physics is also starting to connect attainment, revelation, experimentation, and the changes happening in the world with the consideration of the researcher's inner qualities.

If the researcher is moving or changing inside, that changes the world. It turns out that the sensation of time, space, and spatial movements are our inner coordinates, which do not exist outside of us. They can be different for different people. Therefore, our common understanding depends on how we juxtapose them.

Sometimes we envision light as particles and sometimes as waves. Whether something is moving or not depends on the observer. Is the observer standing or moving? What is happening with all of this?

Scientists have come right up to the boundary of the material world, where everything becomes totally smeared and unclear as to where everything is going. This is unclear to physicists and to psychologists, but they are close to understanding that only a new means of integral attainment of the world will lead us to the next level.

We will attain ourselves and the world precisely when we discover it inside of us. Then we will reach the conclusion that it only appears before us like a mirror, as if it exists outside of us, whereas in reality it is all within us and there is nothing on the outside. Everything that is solid, spatial, and global—all the way until outer space—only seems to exist. But in truth, these are just our own sensations.

When psychologists comprehend that, psychology will become the most important science! We will be able to measure our integral force and accordingly measure the attainment of the world's boundaries and qualities. We will gain control over the functional dependencies between this new, integral organ of perception and what is felt inside of it. This will be the new psychology. It will include all other sciences because man will be placed at the center of this perception.

THE WORLD AS A MIRROR OF OUR IMPERFECTION

– So it turns out that besides me, no one else exists?

– Everything that exists is like a mirror, a reflection of your inner, personal imperfection. Your perfection will be achieved when everything you now feel as external to you will be felt as internal.

– Is it that way specifically to me or is there someone else, for example, you, who imagines this the same way?

– No, I exist only in relation to you and only in order for you to absorb this part that you call me into yourself, so you will completely unite or merge with it, as two drops of water merging into one.

– If I am lying down and doing nothing, then does the world around me simply stop? Or does it "lead its life" regardless?

– The notions of "lead its life" or "stops" do not exist. It depends on what you sense. It is an absolutely individual picture! Physics explains that the observed picture is depicted by the qualities of the observer.

- Why is it so important for me not to be alone in this field, but to be with other subjects who are like me? Why am I so scared of being by myself?

- Because there is a program instilled in you by which you have to reach the absolute integration of the world inside of you. Until you realize this program, the informational genes that emerge in you, which prompt the progress toward integration, will remain unfulfilled. You will not be able to simply lie on the couch and do something unconsciously in order to move the world toward this universal, tighter connection.

Conquests and victories over others are expressions of our demand for a connection. This demand is also revealed through sciences, arts, politics, economics, and anything at all. Of course, these are incorrect forms of integration, but it is integration nonetheless.

ME AND OTHERS BECOME "WE"

- If the perception of the world is infinitely polymorphous, then why is this the correct method out of all others and why does everyone have to use it?

- Because that's how Nature works. It is integral. We are the only ones in Nature who are not integral, meaning the only egoistic creatures. Nature is our cradle, but we exclude ourselves from it and position ourselves outside of it or even above it.

This tiny, insignificant person has the idea that he is destined to conquer, change, and break all of Nature, as if he knew what he was doing. Despite the fact that he is continuously discovering that he does not know anything, and that he is ruining and mutilating everything, he has this feeling.

This method was given to us so that we may reject it and, according to the law of "double negative," conclude that we are the only non-integral part of Nature. Humanity is like a cancerous tumor within Nature, is consuming itself and the entire organism. This is how we treat each other and everything around us, the single organism of Nature.

When we understand what we are really like, we will discover the source and the reason for all the suffering in our human nature. Then we will begin to change it, consciously or unwillingly, under the influence of the problems that will arise.

These problems will become revealed in the near future in all of their horrifying, menacing, and all-enveloping dependence on us, and they will require of us to change. This demand on Nature's part will force us to change. However, we will do it without annihilating the egoistic Nature, but by ascending above it! This is exactly what your friend in India is missing.

There are psychological methods that suppress egoism, turn it off or level it, or put us in a mood as if it doesn't exist, "Let's be like little animals or like plants. Let's live life as if we do not have egoism. Let's play games in a green field and dance around in circles holding hands." All of this is incorrect!

Sometimes I watch performances by national ensembles that are playing an accordion and singing. This is all nice and pretty as a performance at a cultural event, but it cannot be an example for day to day behavior to the masses. These are customs, the inner essence of the nation. But today it cannot be expressed in this way. This is only good onstage at indigenous culture events.

We should not eradicate our egoism and descend to this naïve level. On the contrary, the call of the times is for a constant, enormous growth of egoism and our integration above it.

– A regular person would most likely ask, "But what do I need this for in the practical sense, in the sense of receiving pleasure? What will this give me and my children?"

- The short answer is that you will attain eternity and perfection. And afterwards it is possible to explain the details of it.

By interfacing with everyone else as parts of yourself, you find the missing elements that turn you into an eternal, perfect organism. You lose your small, egoistic "I," but you acquire a tremendous sensation of the only "I" that exists. And what about the others? There are no others. Myself and others turn into "WE," into one, common whole. Then the imperfection, deficiencies, and problems of our world—our current perception—disappear.

PUNISHMENT IS UNNECESSARY IN THE RIGHT SOCIETY

- In life we often encounter situations where a child has to complete an assignment that he does not want to do, but understands that not doing it will inflict punishment. He finds himself clamped between a rock and a hard place, so to speak.

- It is necessary to discriminate with absolute clarity that this approach is incorrect. A child has to be transferred to a different type of clutch: on one hand, society pressures him, and on the other hand, he sees himself and associates himself with society.

There won't be a threat of punishment towering over him. He will understand by himself that otherwise he won't gain social approval, which he so desires. To him precisely this is the method of measuring and evaluating himself, his "I."

On the other hand, we have to give him the ability to control his "clutch," meaning the compulsory corrective force. This is possible if the child understands of his own accord that he has to do the homework or tidy up his room.

Suppose my parents went on vacation and left me at home alone, in charge of the house. But instead of enjoying it, I have to clean up the house because when the parents come home they will punish me if I don't. Therefore, unable to evade punishment, I curse my tiny life and begin to do what I'm expected.

– Or I don't do it at all.

– In this case, everything depends on the punishment. If it is correct, then next time I won't be looking for a way to evade it.

Suppose the punishment forces me to overcome my laziness. That is, the suffering from it has to be greater than the pleasantness of being idle. That is how we try to correct criminals—we punish them so they won't repeat their crime.

But what can we do so the child will understand what kind of assignment Nature, society, or his parents have given him, an understanding by which he will be able to overcome his unwillingness to do what is required of him? Practically speaking, any task comes down to overcoming one's laziness, egoism, the desire to enjoy, and carrying out a task that does not give you any pleasure. Where will I get the energy for that?

The fear of punishment gives me negative energy. The punishment can seem so horrible that I will unwillingly carry out the task while cursing everything in the world.

But it is also possible to create an environment—books and a society—that presents that same work to me in a positive light. For a child, this might be something like a field trip, and for adults— an interesting discovery. This works only if the surrounding society really approves of this task and praises it.

Then the work itself becomes pleasurable. I will not only not get punished, but perhaps the parents will even reward me with a pound of ice-cream. What's important is not this, but the fact that I will receive pleasure because this work is important in the eyes of the people around me. I wouldn't give it up to anyone. I will do it myself because it becomes important to me.

Everything depends on the way in which we create an environment around us that will praise any, even the most difficult, anti-egoistic action to an extent that will give it such importance that we will carry it out with pleasure. And that's how we will advance happily.

To accomplish that, a child must be taught to be a psychologist for himself, and to know how to create the right environment. He will make his life pleasant, even though it will constantly place new problems and barriers before him. But he will view them as levels leading to a higher state that is valued by society.

The problem lies in creating a society around and next to a child that will always help him value anti-egoistic efforts. This is what we have to do, and we have to help every person do this.

– How can we do that? One of my friends has to write a dissertation now because this is necessary for his work and his progress. So should every person in his environment tell him how important this is for the common good?

– Of course! He will sit and write, and will complete the work in two months! You know that it's possible to work on a dissertation for years, or it can be done literally over several months. Everything depends on the inner tension, and you want that tension to be positive.

This is the only way I work. I accumulate the necessary urges that compel me, the gusts that inspire, encourage, and exalt me. And then I start to feel enthusiastic and invigorated, revealing completely new channels of perception, sensation, and ways of expressing things. This is necessary.

You ask me, "How can this be done?" We have to create a small society around every person that will become his tuning fork for correctly attuning himself to these anti-egoistic actions. With its help a person will be able to constantly lift himself. And this will become his inspiration and joy.

CURING MASS DEPRESSION

- Psychology has a notion called an emotional scale where enthusiasm is the expression of the highest and healthiest state.

- Yes, this is the highest state.

- However, the tendency indicates that modern society is becoming immersed in depression and apathy, which is the lowest state on this scale.

- This is Nature's call to us: to create a society or a nucleus that could serve as a model of unification and ascent for us. Otherwise we will all simply lie down and become immobile.

A few days ago I heard a report by Russia's chief of the health ministry where he stated that over the next 10-15 years half of Russia's population will be depressed. These are not some journalist's surmises, but an open statement by the chief of the health ministry!

We can only imagine what kind of problems there are in reality. If the chief of the health ministry says that half of the population will be depressed in 10-15 years, it means that there are already a lot of depressed people.

Today, concealed depression is everywhere. It doesn't depend on how developed a society is or on the standard of living. It doesn't depend on anything. We are observing a process of the transition of depression from a concealed form into an apparent form because the integral interconnection of all of Nature's elements is becoming openly revealed in our world, while we are unable to become similar to it.

We have to be integrally interconnected, to be a single humanity all together. But in the meantime, we are horrible individualists. This opposition to one another evokes cruel sensations within us. We will have to become aware of them and solve this problem.

THE MODEL OF SANCTITY

- Almost every person considers something "sacred." It can be a flag or an army regiment's banner. It's the concept of something that's sacred and immovable. Is there anything in this method that can be called sacred?

- People have always had a need for this. They declared statues, trees, and stones sacred, or some adult or child. There has always been a need for a model that might even be nameless. In reality, this is the necessity to reveal the upper force, God, the Creator, something higher.

Today this need is not expressed so clearly, but it is still there. The religions are not dying out. They're going into hiding for a time, and then they will rise back to the surface and even to the forefront of life. Religions in their normal and fanatic form are yet to become expressed. This is still ahead of us.

What needs to become sacred in human society is integration, our total equivalence with Nature. If we attain *that*, we will enter a state where nothing can harm us or touch us, nothing can move us from this perfect and eternal level.

When we enter that level, all of Nature will become included in us. We will completely close circuit it inside of us and perceive it as one eternal, perfect, and infinite whole. The problems of life and death will disappear, as well as the hardships and suffering because we won't exist individually, but in the common, analog, integral system. This model is exactly what has to become sacred.

What does sacred mean? Do I have to experience any movement I make from the standpoint of how can I create, find, and form one more action inside of me for the sake of realizing this model? How can I help others—to the extent that I perceive them as existing outside of me—to see this model, understand it, and agree that this is our only correct future state? This is sanctity—the future, perfect state of humanity, which we can create today on our o– Can we play with this sacred thing in some way?

– It is created within us! It is not you or me, or someone else, but what we all create together. We do not draw some kind of little god or something that's unacceptable to others, yet pleasant for our egoism. We create the Absolute! We create this higher force above us, and *we are it.*

AN ANECDOTE IS A PARADOXICAL EXPRESSION OF INTEGRATION

– You once said that you like verbal games in the form of anecdotes.

– Yes, just not crude ones, but ones that are built upon the unexpected combination of opposite parts which in principle should not connect. The ability to connect things that are not connectable is a special mental quality.

Some people have souls consisting of two opposites and they aspire to connect these opposites into a single, integral form. These people are special, and if you hear them tell an anecdote, then it's a real anecdote. All the others are crude surrogates.

– Can we use this form in our method so children will make up good stories of their own and tell them to one another?

– Yes. But they shouldn't be mundane stories about a husband, a wife, and their lovers. They should not include insults and widespread clichés. The challenge is to find two opposites and to unite them in spite of our routine notions.

– From what age can these verbal games be used among children? When are they ready for this?

– I don't think it should be done in early age because this requires very serious inner development and life experience, the ability to tell anecdotes apart from jokes or camouflaged insults, and from aggression and slander that play on man's darkest instincts and therefore seem pleasant to him. But these are not anecdotes.

An anecdote is a story that combines opposites in a completely unexpected way, turning them around to reveal some special aspect, uncovering the interface, unity, and integration between them. An anecdote is an unexpected expression of integration.

Theatre as a Means to Fight Egoism

- We Are Always on Stage
- Acting Skills
- Collective Games with Egoism
- The Right Age for Studying Acting
- Not Playing Fairy Tales, But Real Life
- Becoming Objective through Acting
- From an Amorphous "I" to a Reliable "We"
- Why Theatre Shows Were Ridiculed
- Unity Brings People to the "Human" Level
- The Actor Becomes the Stage Director
- Not All the Roles Must Be Played
- The Most Intense Sensations Come from a Deficiency
- The Goal: Integral Humanity

Let's talk about the role of acting in the method of integral upbringing. You often say that a child, like any person, should learn to change himself, to develop the ability to work above his states.

– A person has to learn to play various roles, and in this way, present himself to others in a different guise than he really is.

– I noticed that everyone has the ability to act, not just actors. What is the essence of this human quality?

WE ARE ALWAYS ON STAGE

– Of course, we are all acting. After all, we don't know how to behave. Animals behave naturally. They don't have feelings of shame or envy. True, they do experience biological envy, if you can call an animal's emotions that. This feeling they have is determined by biological factors. Animals behave however Nature has programmed them to behave.

But man's desire is on a higher level. He works hard trying to earn social approval, respect, and honor. It's as if he is working for others in order to receive knowledge and various privileges from them. Man wishes to feel his power over others who are like him, and he is compelled to act in front of them. He cannot allow himself the freedom to express his natural qualities. Our inborn qualities would turn us into a mere herd of animals. But when a person acts (which is what we all do), then it's no longer a herd. It's a human society.

By performing different roles, we turn the herd into a human society. It is how we differ from animals. We are always acting out some persona and never behave the way we really are, even when we are alone.

The more humanity develops, the more it engages in tighter communication and people constantly follow examples they see in others. That way, we are all like actors, scanning inside through the roles we've observed in others and "putting them on" when the right circumstance arises. This is how we behave. It is natural for each of us. Sometimes we notice this in others, such as when teenagers take famous Hollywood actors as role models and try to emulate the popular characters they have played.

But the skill of acting is something different. An actor plays a role consciously rather than unconsciously, unlike a regular person who has collected various examples since childhood and simply imitates the behavior of others.

At a specific stage we begin to understand that man's task is to come to total integration, to become as one man, to feel each of us as part of a certain entirely coordinated natural mechanism.

For that, man has to feel the nature of others and "play along" with them. Obviously, it's not an accident that man was endowed with the ability to act. Every person has to feel and understand everyone else. And for that, I have to fully agree with the existence of something that's opposite to my natural qualities.

I am a small, primitive egoist who constantly wants to "hog" everything to himself. But to conform to society so that I may properly connect with it, I have to become an actor.

So it's wonderful that I act out other people. My own nature pushes me to force everyone to do what I want, even when I don't *know* what it is that I want.

But for an artist, it is important to do the opposite and learn from *other* people. It's important for him to be able to adapt his qualities to others and play along with them, and this does not diminish the person in the slightest. On the contrary, it is how he connects with the environment and rises to a higher level. Thus, one studies people and comes closer to them, developing the ability to be in the right communication with them.

ACTING SKILLS

One more special quality of acting is that when a person comes close to being in contact with the environment, he "comes out" of his current problems and qualities.

Suppose I am experiencing some personal drama. To position myself correctly in relation to the environment, I must be in a different state. This means I have to "come out of myself," forget about my own worries, and "put on" a different role. And in that new form, I proceed to work with the collective.

By working this way, I will gradually be able to resolve my conflicts to some extent and understand their cause, and absorb or add to myself the desires and aspirations of other people, which caused the conflict between us. The conflicts might remain for some time, in which case at some point in the future I will remember this conflict and will be able to understand it, to become included in it, and to experience the state of its participants.

A person can "come out" of his nature and enter another role. He can literally dissolve in it, completely detach from the troubles for some time, however tragic. These are the opportunities we can learn from actors.

COLLECTIVE GAMES WITH EGOISM

Everything in the work of an actor is aimed at giving a person the ability to become included in others, to transcend his egoism.

I play with my egoism in a way that I come out of it and enter an altruistic role, becoming it. In this role I feel other people, what they are truly like. I learn to connect with them. And all of this becomes possible thanks to me rising above myself.

One has to learn to play the roles of everyone, and then, as it is written, "Habit will become second nature." Gradually, we will see how beneficial this is and will desire to be in this state, in the right communication.

– This exit from oneself is very clear to me. When it happens, the sensation is astounding. But what do you mean by "the right communication"?

– We have to discover our absolute connection. The laws of commutation in an integral system are very simple. Each of us has his own nature. And he has to create such a field of understanding around him that through it he will be able to connect with others. We all have to do it. To the extent that every person creates this shell around him, finding the widest contact with the people around him, he will become corrected and will operate properly.

The efficiency of every element in society is achieved when a person keeps only his basic, initial, fundamental quality, his "I." This initial quality we have is very small. All the other qualities in a person must be aimed only at enabling this "I" to connect with everyone else and work for the sake of others' desires and qualities, for the purpose of building a connection with them.

It's like a mother goose that is surrounded by 15 goslings. She thinks and cares for each of them. The little geese walk in front of their mom, and she treads behind them. Each of them is in her field of vision, and she makes contact with all of them.

That is how a person should position himself in relation to the environment, understanding every person's desires, aspirations, thoughts, and worries. He should help all of these people make their dreams come true. Like any well working mechanism, we can only operate when all of the parts are in total agreement.

THE RIGHT AGE FOR STUDYING ACTING

– When a person creates a certain new facet within himself, he discovers how multi-faceted he is. How many facets can there be in a person? And at what age can this be taught to a child?

– This cannot be taught to very young children because the "herd feeling" is not expressed in them before the age of 3. Until age 3 their little individuality does not imagine that there is someone else outside of them, with other needs. At that age a child does not communicate and is aimed only at reception.

But between the ages of 3-6, children develop the rudimentary understanding of bestowal and interaction. Between ages 6-9, this understanding is strengthened and remains that way for the rest of their lives. During this delicate age, Nature offers us a unique opportunity to instill in a child the right attitude toward the environment.

– Is it possible to teach this to a child through acting?

– This is what we are trying to do. We understand that this act has to be two-sided. And I want children to be taught the skill of acting in the framework of our educational association.

We have to show a child that it is possible to come out of himself and ascend above his own qualities. At first, children can tune out of their problems and worries in this way. And later we teach them a different role. A child is like an actor with his own inner world: First he learns the role that he has to play, and then he starts playing it. Why? A person creates his own inner image of the other person and studies how to interact with it correctly, learning to enter the reality of the other person.

To this end it is good to teach children the art of acting professionally. In our studies children are already playing these roles, trying to enter the characters of their friends. That way they start to understand each other better and become part of something common. The shared character of the whole group starts to live in every one of them.

– Is it best for a child to act out the character of one of their friends specifically, or is it also possible to work with other images that are more removed from them?

– It's necessary to work on all of the phenomena in the children's field of vision.

NOT PLAYING FAIRY TALES, BUT REAL LIFE

– Which boundaries can we delineate here? Can children play animals or plants? Or should they only play people?

– It's best to play people. Why should they play animals? This just brings relics of ancient notions to the surface, like talking trees, or the sun talking to the moon, or a wolf to a fox.

Within the framework of our upbringing, these types of fairy tales, and actually anything that brings a person down to a lower level is harmful. It not only gives us an incorrect idea of the animate world, but of the world in general.

We should understand our unique position. Animals are on a different level of development. They are not people. We shouldn't idolize or personify trees, animals, or mechanical toys, such as when a mechanical toy with a human face suddenly starts moving around and talking.

We have to treat a child like an adult. On the inside a child is an adult. He looks at us with the eyes of an adult rather than a child. Sometimes mature, serious memories of childhood awaken in us. These reminiscences remain in us for the rest of our lives and still determine our attitude to life today.

Unfortunately, the talking trees, sun, or choo choo trains we saw in childhood will always remain in our subconscious. This is exactly why we cannot look at life seriously. It holds us back in some way. We continue to act out a kind of fairy tale within us and do not live for real.

– Can a 10 year old play a grandfather?

– Yes. To be able to have the right contact with people, he has to act out men and women of all ages.

– The first thing I noticed when I started working with a group of teenagers was their desire to be on stage as fast as possible, to be applauded, and to earn something as fast as possible. Should this aspiration be suppressed, meaning, should we try to make them focus on the practical work?

– A person cannot develop without positive emotions such as rewards, presents, and honors. We are egoists. If a child worked hard and performed beautifully, the collective must appreciate it and reward him with applause, to show him its approval.

But we have to help a child choose the right aspiration, one that will enable him to receive that reward. Maybe their work should be videotaped and then analyzed—whose role turned out best and why? For example, you can videotape ten boys when each of them is playing his neighbor, and the neighbor is playing the next person.

BECOMING OBJECTIVE THROUGH ACTING

I did not study the basics of acting, but everything in an actor's work is aimed toward creating the right communication. This is natural. When we play the roles of our friends, we understand each other better and as a result, the amount of conflicts immediately drops. Statistics show this as well. A person starts to judge everyone, including himself and his friend. Besides his own role, he can learn one more role and live out both. He can become his own judge, or his friend's advocate. These persona become totally equal! By acting, a person becomes objective.

– During the workshops, should we monitor the extent to which the children have learned to understand and justify one another?

– Of course. If I start living out someone else's role, it means that I justify that person to the end. I blame myself entirely. This is natural. I "enter" him, so I am he and he is me.

Suppose that a conflict arose in one of our groups. The children's egoism suddenly and drastically escalated, and they could not do anything about it. During the studies they listen to articles about friendship and unification in order to achieve a common goal, and they sing and communicate. Everything's normal. And then suddenly, a minute later, there is an explosion of egoism and conflicts break out as if the children have been replaced by someone else. And half an hour later, at another lesson, friendly relations are restored between them.

What can we do so these outbursts of egoism won't occur? How can we prevent the egoism from breaking out to the surface, so separation won't emerge? The children admit that they cannot control these outbursts.

So what do we plan on doing? First of all, videotape the entire process on camera, including the mutual criticism and accusations. This will allow us to see pride, envy, the desire for power over others, and in general, all of the feelings and urges that are inherent in every person. Then we will show it to the kids. Let each of them try to play the role of his friend.

Suppose you and I quarreled, it was filmed, and now we are watching this process from the side. At first, I am 100% sure that I am right, and I live out my role all over again. We remember what we experienced.

But the teacher says, "Let each of you learn about the other person's behavior and try to understand why he acted that way." So now I have to look at the whole process through the eyes of my friend, I have to exit myself and enter your state. I have to see myself "from within you," how you see me, how and why you are blaming me, and what you are criticizing me for. After that I have to play the role of my friend, and the friend plays me.

We know that this is not easy for children. Afterwards we discuss to what extent we succeeded in playing the first role and the second one. Thus, your first character, which participated in the conflict in reality, becomes just one of two roles. You look at your first state more objectively, your position shifts, and you are already somewhere between these two images.

And it doesn't matter if everything doesn't work out perfect right away. The most important thing is that as a result, the child's qualities begin to gain a "multi-faceted" character. He begins to understand that it is possible to be different and that it is possible to learn to rise above himself.

In a child, egoistic outbursts are expressed powerfully and occur immediately. But we help the children learn to transcend them.

– Onstage, egoism agrees with this kind of work.

– With playing a different role?

– Yes. And does it! It's a huge pleasure.

– And we don't need anything more than that.

– But during moments of real outbursts, it is very difficult to negotiate with egoism.

– It's not that difficult, really. This is exactly how children start taking part in the process of working on egoism. Let them sit in a semi-circle in front of their friends and act. And the more a child can rise above being a slave to his egoism, and put on a different role from the bottom of his heart, change "places" with his friend, the more approval he will earn from his society.

By living out foreign images and drawing any one of them out as if from a deck of cards, a child begins to treat these roles "objectively" so he no longer personally identifies with any of them.

A child's attitude to his "I" changes. He asks the question, "What has remained in him of this 'I'?" A person begins to realize that he is pure and not filled with anything. He begins to see everything as purely an act. That way, a person even starts treating his own urges as phenomena that are installed into him by some program.

FROM AN AMORPHOUS "I" TO A RELIABLE "WE"

– And what is our real "I"?

– Our real "I" is completely amorphous. It does not have any image.

– It is integral?

– No. Integrality forces us to be in some kind of roles or images all the time. But our original desire does not have any form.

– In pedagogy there is a technique called "the mask of aggression" where an adult pretends to be angry, but in reality he is treating the child kindly. Should a child really experience a certain feeling, for example, anger, or should he learn to act out these feelings?

– This depends on the children's age. Of course, before 11 or 12, or maybe before age 13, they cannot be in different inner and external images simultaneously. At this age a person is not that multi-faceted yet. But then again, a lot depends on practice. If the children constantly try to express themselves in new forms, they will be able to do it at an earlier age as well. And there's no doubt that in adolescence they can already be in several multi-layered roles, and change these masks very quickly.

– Shouldn't they identify themselves with these states?

– This act is not self-deceit. They don't lie to other people by doing it. A person conforms himself to the work of the common mechanism, society, in order to bring it to harmony.

What's the point of thinking, "I was created this way and that's all. I don't change; let everyone conform to me; let others break themselves"? In the end, this won't give a person anything. So what kind of communication would result from that? How would a person be able to feel and experience his real, higher self? He wouldn't.

– So that means that we are nevertheless teaching a child to be in several states simultaneously?

– We are teaching the children to "dress up" in different forms, as if they are transfiguring. Every child will accumulate these roles within him, will be able to work with them, understand what he experiences, and see that nothing is positive or negative, but everything is relative. The "I" exists only in order to connect with others.

Thus, on the inside, every person accumulates roles, abilities, understanding, and most important, a new level of communication.

– In every transfiguration, any role, an actor stays in control of himself. During the act he always keeps a certain sensation that he is looking at himself from above, so to say. Is this correct? Or should he try to give himself over to the role completely and lose his self-control, trying to come out of himself to the maximum?

– I don't think we can demand everything from the children all at once. At first we should give them just one assignment. Gradually, as they get used to playing various roles, place secondary and tertiary tasks before them. For example, first you have to enter someone's character and continue being in control of yourself, playing a dual role.

Within the mechanism we are discussing, a person has to communicate with all the other people in the world. For that he has to feel them so strongly that through them he will feel a third and a fourth plane.

I act you out, "dressing" into you. And to do that I study your personality and your qualities. This way, by internally experiencing your character, I imagine how you relate to your children, for example. And that is already a third plane. And so on.

– Different children have different talents, and their abilities to act are not the same. This kind of transfiguration is easy for one person but difficult for another. Should we make the children equal or separate them? For example, should the especially gifted children study in one group and the ones who find acting more difficult be placed in another?

– A group has to be a group, and its progress has to be cohesive. A child should become accustomed to it. Gradually, the children will change, become accustomed to one another, and learn to understand each other. That's how they will grow—together.

This kind of development is programmed in all of humanity. We should not change this or create some sort of universal or artificial groups. All of this scares a child very much, depriving him of confidence and the chance to develop.

– What should we do if one child finds it pleasant and easy to enter another character, while another is embarrassed and has difficultly overcoming that feeling?

– A child will learn by being next to the able friends. The entire process has to be aimed toward his friends drawing him into the act and helping him. This depends on the educator. And it doesn't matter if the child starts out by playing secondary roles. As he learns, he will advance.

I don't think the group should be divided into those who are better and those who are worse. When children conjoin into larger groups (groups of 20, 30, or more, instead of 10), they will become sort of a mini-society that includes diverse people of different personalities.

WHY THEATRE SHOWS WERE RIDICULED

– If acting is so important for man's development, why was it so ridiculed and even persecuted for so many centuries? Some people were even burned at the stake for it.

– Actors were always ridiculed. They only became respected in our "progressive" era. Humanity does not have the right approach to creating a connection between us. We connect through our egoism. We don't do it through interference, but however each of us finds it most convenient for himself. We connect through a kind of buffer: "I give to you and you give to me." That's how we buy, sell, and exchange pleasantries. Depending on our age and other factors, we change the levels of our status, power, and force.

From every direction we establish the maximum possible egoistic contact, while keeping a certain distance as a safety net against unexpected turns in our relationships, even noticing the changes in one's intonation. It controls us from within. And humanity automatically followed this principle, which enabled every person to define his place right away. It works as if we are a herd of animals where each specimen knows it place and function. It knows when it can or cannot do something. And the exact same thing happens in the human society. Because we are egoists, we act by the same principle.

But when acting appears, it becomes unclear. Who are these people? Are they commoners or lords? Are they strong or weak? Are they good or bad? Or maybe they are bandits? One's individuality is lost, depriving us of the ability to form normal, egoistic communication.

In the past everything was clearly delineated. People aspired to put everyone in their fixed places—you are a psychologist so you have to wear a black shirt, for example, and it can't be otherwise.

People even settled in different places depending on their professions, their guild. You had to live at the street you were appointed to and choose a wife from a specific circle. Your family had to abide by a set pattern of life, and your hat and attire had to have a specific cut, with no other options. Everything was prescribed, down to the food people ate, absolutely everything. You were even told, "This will be your cemetery."

Everything was clear—who lives where, his origin, who he is allowed to come into contact with, and from whom he should stay away.

But actors mixed all of that up. They made fun of and laughed at everyone. Some puny little actor was acting as if he were a prince! This was admissible only if people would internalize the idea that the work of an actor is the lowest of all the possible professions, immoral and plebeian.

During the necessitated division of society, especially during the Middle Ages, no one could even think about developing their contacts or making other people understand them. Everyone had to be perfectly obedient. The most that was allowed was for strangers to dance a minuet together.

But today everything is the opposite. We have to communicate with one another the right way. And for that, we have to learn to "enter" the characters of other people.

We have to understand that humanity had to go through all of its phases in order to reach the current phase. Today, we have to break all the limits of the past and form the right social communication. And for that, a person has to learn to play the characters of other people.

UNITY BRINGS PEOPLE TO THE "HUMAN" LEVEL

– The constant act really does engross an actor. This brings him great pleasure, but at the same time, an agonizing feeling arises where you lose your self. How can one get rid of it?

– You don't need to search for yourself. Go ahead, lose yourself. Feel yourself only when you make contact with other people and understand them.

– It doesn't matter whom? After all, people have the most diverse personalities.

– We are talking about a society where all the people already aspire to include the qualities of others in them. Their aspiration to this is the beginning of the human fellowship.

If everyone wants to become included in everyone, then something common is formed. This is the result of our combination, our attempts to come out of ourselves and unite. This state is called "mutual guarantee" and it means that everyone is "in one heart," one desire, one *intention*.

When a person begins to discern this common quality, then his own "I" goes into hiding and practically disappears. Then, a new quality emerges.

There is no me or you or him. Something singular and whole forms above us, composed of all three of us. But it is not the sum of our three qualities. It is one quality.

If we begin to feel our unity to this extent, in it, we will feel a new, higher dimension. Only this level of development is called "the human level." Today we are still in the egoistic, animate state. But unity brings people to the state called "human."

On this level, we begin to feel the integral, global, holistic nature. We acquire the sensation of eternal and perfect life, separating from all of our problems, our restless and agonizing states, and impulsive urges. A person becomes included in something different and new.

THE ACTOR BECOMES THE STAGE DIRECTOR

– When a person becomes a professional actor and becomes absorbed in the new way of life, he begins to fear many things.

The image of Mephistopheles (the devil) immediately emerges in his subconscious. Why does this fear emerge?

– A person is afraid of losing himself. By being immersed in a certain role, sometimes he feels that if he stays there a minute longer, he won't be able to go back anymore.

These fears and apprehensions are well-warranted. A person's psychological structure is not balanced and it is possible to completely reformat the behavioral program that's operating in it, like in a computer. If a different program is inserted there, a person can forget about everything and behave differently. These practices and methods are applied by power structures in various countries in the world.

Our children are clearly aware that they work for the sake of understanding their friend, for the sake of feeling his nature. To accomplish this, I become included in the qualities of my friend, and create his image within me. And my friend does the same in relation to me. Thus, there will be two images in me and two images in him. This enables us to communicate correctly, and to begin to understand on another. This is why we are acting.

The fact that we can to understand each other today does not mean that we will understand each other tomorrow. Our mutual understanding must constantly be renewed. Tomorrow we will have a new egoism because it constantly grows. Our moods will change, as well as many other things around us, such as the circumstances in our families, and the relationships with our friends at school. All of this will influence our personalities. Changes happen all the time.

This kind of work in a team, where we observe one another, criticize or encourage each other's work, enables us to accumulate an enormous collection of analytical instruments and look at the entire process from the side, no longer through the eyes of an actor who is trying on different roles, but through the eyes of the stage director. Just as Nature orders us around and plays with us, I, too, begin to see this game. I develop a very sensible attitude to what is happening and begin to understand that life is but an act of various roles.

Therefore, if children work on a certain situation with their friends and observe their behaviors together, I don't think any problems will arise.

- Is it possible to try playing the role of the stage director as well?

- We are talking about children, and young children at that. When they turn about 7 or 8, egoism begins to manifest in them in a severe manner. That is when we should gradually start introducing elements of acting, "Try to be in his position now, and he will be in yours. Remember how he yelled at you yesterday, and now you try to play that role."

Is it possible to direct or manage this process at this age? I do not rule out this possibility. It depends on how long the group has been studying and what skills it has acquired.

- Every time a scene is acted out, even if it's the same scene, it turns out differently.

- This is apparent, especially when playing out the same roles.

- Should children repeat the same scenes over and over again?

- This will happen anyway.

- What can we learn from that?

- In this process, children will be constantly studying themselves. I think it is necessary to videotape everything that is happening to them, watch it, and let the children evaluate what they saw, and then repeat it.

A child begins to see how relative his behavior and opinion are, that there is nothing absolute about them. What is absolute is the single, unified whole that is created when they all unite. And together we will build the Absolute. But whatever exists in each of us—it always changes.

NOT *ALL* THE ROLES MUST BE PLAYED

– Actors don't like to play psychologically unstable people or to experience death on stage. When working with children, how can we define the boundaries of which roles are admissible?

– Children should only portray the characters of the people whom they need to come in contact with. This can be a prince or a pauper, a wealthy person or a poor one, an evildoer or a righteous person, a man or a woman, it doesn't matter.

But they don't have to enter other characters. I have to understand every person I am in contact with in our society—be it a child, an adult, or an old man. I have to learn to play their states within me and acquire their characters.

– So a child shouldn't play a person who has died, for example?

– Why should he come in contact with someone who has died? What would be the point of that? Or, for example, why should he have to communicate with a very young child?

Of course, contact with an infant is possible. But usually infants are cared for by their mothers. She understands the baby instinctively. This is how one animal understands another one in Nature. They are practically one organism, and a mother exhibits the animate feeling towards a child.

To understand the relationship between a child and a mother, we have to become included in them and we have to play out these states. But for that, we don't have to have contact with an infant because there is a mother for that.

However, I do have to understand all the other people and as a result, accumulate the whole world, all of humanity, within me.

– Should a child play various life situations rather than abstract things? Should he portray a real fear rather than an abstract one?

– What kind of abstract fear can there be?

– A child can see something in a movie, for example.

– Life is full of real images and impressions. It's necessary to teach a child the right understanding and the right way to join every life situation and every incident he encounters.

How does a child find the right way to communicate with a specific group of people who are from a specific social sector? Or how does he understand himself? Who is he? Let him act out himself. It seems to him that he is always in himself, inside the nature that is his. But let him imagine the opposite.

I am the stage director, and this stage director is observing me acting out "me." This makes me look at myself critically at how I express my "I". It's as if two planes begin to coexist within me.

It turns out that this is the only way I can communicate even with my self. This is the only way I can understand myself.

Maybe actors are taught to act in other ways, probably using specific professional terms. I am not familiar with the basics of acting; I am speaking about it the way I understand this process, the way I see it.

We have to get to know man's nature. We are only now starting to realize that we are all egoists and do not see or feel others. But in order to save our civilization, we have to become similar to Nature and become integrally connected.

Acting or playing is very important for a person's development. To rise from one level to the next, I have to literally act out the next level. This is how a child portrays a pilot or a chauffeur, for example, and when he becomes an adult he really does become one of them. Playing is instilled in us by Nature.

The same thing happens in our workshops. When I play other people, it's as if I become them and their characters enter me. That is how a person accumulates the whole world within him.

THE MOST INTENSE SENSATIONS
COME FROM A DEFICIENCY

– I find it much more interesting to play negative characters. They touch me more, while the positive ones turn out boring. Since these roles influence us so much, how should we treat them?

– Negative images, sad music, and tragic events are always more vivid than positive ones, which seem flat to us. This is clear because a person is the desire to enjoy. As a result, our most intense sensations come from a lack of something. When pleasure comes to a person, he considers it obvious: "As an egoist, this is what I deserve, so I don't feel the pleasure that intensely. But a lack of something, which I deserve but don't have, is something I feel very intensely." This is how egoism evaluates itself—one-sidedly, with a slant toward the sensation of a deficiency.

Which roles should children play, positive or negative? Questions about this should not arise. I have to play the role however it is. A person must first dissect the entire character into fragments, and then try to analyze them as objectively as possible, choosing the most indicative ones and learning to reproduce them, to create these situations within him, to become a stage director, and then to express them.

For example, I am asked to play Johnny. That means I have to remember what circumstances I met him in, recall his personality traits, how he moves, and everything that is typical of Johnny. I have to understand what appeals to me and what I don't like. I have to discern all of this in relation to my egoism.

– What if I don't like something? Do I have to try to justify these qualities and agree with them?

– The most important thing is to act them out. It's very important to recall the character very distinctly, what it's like, and what it is. When a person starts to play the role and enters the character, he feels his new attitude to what is happening. Then a person involuntarily agrees with how his prototype behaved in this situation. By playing any role, I come closer to the person I play.

– There's even an expression, "falling in love with your character."

THE GOAL: INTEGRAL HUMANITY

We scrupulously analyze any situation or any character, then act them out and experience them, and they remain in a person. Tens or perhaps hundreds of such characters comprise the communicative mechanism that enables a person to connect to the world. A person becomes multi-faceted and multi-layered in his understanding of any person, and can therefore make contact with anyone.

This understanding is not in order to manipulate people or to find profit from communicating with them, nor is it for finding a convenient, egoistic way to position one's "I" by the principle of "a lady who's pleasant in all respects."

We say that the most important thing is a person's ability to bring every character to life in his "I." That is how he will come in contact with all of humanity, creating a single whole. Then, each of us will create a "field" of characters around him, by which we will achieve the integral humanity.

That is how the human society gradually develops to the point where every person is comprised of all the people who exist. Also, this process is not difficult. Psychologists know that there are not that many prototypes of people. How many have psychologists enumerated?

– Twenty.

– So what's the problem? If a person adopts these characters, through them he will be able to understand and come into contact with any person. He will understand me too. He will see me in a good light and will be well-disposed toward me. Thus, we will evoke a good, favorable integration in the world.

– Who should teach children acting? Can famous actors be invited to do it? Or, can children be instructed by other children who are 2 or 3 years older?

– I don't think that older kids will be able to manage this process. This kind of work requires a mature individual. I am sure that even the best actors and directors won't be able to direct the work in our classrooms unless they understand our objectives. Professional mastery is not so important to us.

First of all, every action made by our educators has to have a clear objective: to understand the friends, unite with them in the right way, and create a common whole with them.

An outsider won't be able to help us because these tasks are simply not in his field of vision. The most important thing for a professional actor is a convincing, realistic act. But that doesn't matter to us. Not every child will be able to express himself fully and poignantly. And this is not necessary.

But instead, our children will gradually begin to understand what they should aspire to and what opportunities are opening up to them. They will bring their desire to its logical completion and will begin to understand one anotherThey remember their natural behavior in a specific situation, and each of them plays the role of his friend. After that they return to their initial characters and reproduce their natural behavior.

For example, I blame you for something and you blame me. Now each of us has to play the role of the opponent. Then I once again return to my natural qualities, acting out the initial situation.

Children collect all these images inside of them and discuss how it will help them to unite, to become an integral humanity.

I begin to understand the nature of my friend, and he begins to understand mine. That is how we ascend above our nature and decide how we can unite all of our qualities. The conclusion of this discussion is the most important part of our work.

Every person has to include the whole world within him.

A THERAPEUTIC PROGRAM FOR SOCIETY

- Learning from History
- Saving Civilization
- Upbringing on TV
- How to Realize the Method
- Self- Education for Children and Adults
- Practice, Example, and Interaction
- Upbringing for Juvenile Delinquents
- A Healing Program for Society

LEARNING FROM HISTORY

We draw on ancient sources to form the foundations of this method. These sources were created in Ancient Babylon, where the same problem appeared for the first time: incorrect egoistic connections emerged in an integral society.

The residents of Babylon planned to collaborate in order to build a tower as high as the sky, but soon discovered that they could not understand one another. The confusion and the mixing of tongues is the lack of understanding of one another by many egoists.

Josephus Flavius wrote about it in a very interesting way. Three million people (back then this was the entire civilization) lived on a small territory, bound by the Tigris and Euphrates rivers. Having abundant sun and water, people grew barley, wheat, and garlic, and caught fish. Their food contained all of the necessary elements. These were wonderful conditions for an ancient civilization. But all of a sudden, the residents of Babylon couldn't stand being together. As a result, they drifted apart in every direction. Every family, clan, and guild went in different directions and founded nations. But back then there was room for them to disperse from one another, and by doing that they were able to pacify their state of separation.

Today we are in the same situation. We are building our civilization like that "tower as high as the sky," wishing to consume everything. We are draining the last drops of what the earth has to offer—minerals, metals, coal, petroleum, and gas. But at the end of the tube that humanity has inserted into the earth, emptiness is starting to glare back at us.

And we understand that we are facing the end because the civilization we have built does not have anything to sustain it anymore.

Thus, a very serious question arises: What are we doing!? How can we come to our senses? How can we educate people ahead of time, before the end arrives?

SAVING CIVILIZATION

We have to show humanity that the end is already near. If only humanity could peek into this tube and see that it's empty! Petroleum, gas, and water cannot be replaced with solar or nuclear power plants. A car travels ten kilometers on a liter of gas. And we don't have any other fuel or energy that fits into a liter of liquid and can produce this kind of result. In other words, our civilization is petroleum based, and with petroleum gone, our civilization will end as well!

The only thing we need is to immediately reduce our consumption to the minimal level. We have to use the remaining resources only to provide the vital necessities. No one will starve or give up necessary things. People will lead a normal existence! The average modern family has to have an apartment, a job for all its members, and the means to raise and educate the children.

We have to inculcate the ideology of voluntary restriction from the bottom to the top. This includes feeding the hungry and lowering the standard of living of the wealthy to a normal level. Practically, this is socialism. But who will agree to it? What kind of suffering will be able to force us to redistribute all of the available resources, to make all members of society equal, to unite us with each other, and to establish the right interactions between them?

To arrive at such a system, we have to start feeling our absolute dependence on one another like one family. The contemporary person completely lacks this sensation and is completely indifferent to it. He has no need for a family, for children, relatives, or friends. His only interest is to have a good time during the period Nature has allotted him for his existence, called "life."

Do we have time to work on upbringing? This is a long-term process that requires an entire system to be created. Unfortunately, we are under time constraints because in the next 10-15 years we will completely use up the remaining resources and then there won't be anything left.

These are the data from published and unpublished research.

Therefore, our method of integral upbringing is first of all addressed to the parents. We are counting on man's natural instinct to save his children. Let's turn them into people! Let's prepare them for this inevitable, necessary, future interaction of every person with everyone!

A person who enters integration correctly will benefit from it. He won't just be well brought up, but will have the necessary skills for survival because it's not the strongest who will survive, since there won't be anything to snatch from one another. Survival will depend on one's ability to adapt, to understand that integration, interconnection, mutual guarantee, concessions, connections, and unification is Nature's call. And Nature's goal is to bring humanity to equilibrium.

This system has to be developed in every language on the internet. There is no other solution. And first and foremost, it must address the parents because children are our future. Children who are 10 years old today will be that new humanity. We have to do everything for their sake.

I think that the only solution is to address man's natural, egoistic desire to provide his children with a reliable program for life. Simply throwing this out to the people would be like shouting out in the desert. But when we address parents, we touch a sensitive point to which they can relate.

UPBRINGING ON TV

– You have a wholesome, harmonious method that is based on ancient sources and laws of Nature. We are already seeing the results of it on children who are being brought up in your system. But this is still many miles away from "the people." How can we deliver your method to parents the world over?

– I think we have to create TV programs because there is a TV set in every home. There should be a channel that is free of charge, which will constantly broadcast interesting, pleasant-to-watch programs.

This kind of channel is also favorable for the authorities and wealthy people because it will calm people down, make them friendlier, and will lower tensions. It is aimed at raising children and it answers the public demand in some sense, the public's desire to bring back the positive elements of a socialistic society. It won't require any redistribution on the part of the authorities at this moment, and it will be aimed only at upbringing.

We are not talking about the fact that today we are already starting to redistribute property and make it accessible to the entire population or the whole world. We are saying that it is necessary to raise people in the spirit of friendship, cooperation, and unity. This position cannot have any official opponents (although of course, certain nationalist movements can always see this as conflicting with their ideas, but they are very insignificant forces).

This is a sure-fire idea! It is natural! And it doesn't involve any coercion! We will implement it in life only to the extent that people are required to unite in order to survive (and we will see this over the next few years). Before that happens, we simply hear, understand, and study it, similar to how a student studies for 5 or 6 years prior to beginning to work and applying the knowledge.

– We have been talking openly about this method for several months now and there are already a lot of people who are interested in it, including famous scientists, academics, and world-recognized specialists. They want to actively collaborate with us. Should we interact with them?

- Of course! Where are these people? What would they like to hear from me? I am ready to speak to everyone, to explain and develop the method, because in principle, I am alone for now. But interaction with other people, especially from other fields of research, could help to clarify and supplement what's needed.

HOW TO REALIZE THE METHOD

- Is it necessary to bring this method to every person? Also, who should carry out this task—perhaps artists, scientists, and educators? And what means can we use?

- We can make documentaries and movies on this topic, produce plays, create television programs and computer games. We have to hold panel games and debates on this topic on TV and in the press.

Because this method talks about the society of the future and the format of that society, it can encompass any layers of society. There are various ways of implementing it and showing it to a person. I think that we have to get the government interested in this as well.

This can be done by the people who bring their ideas to the top through memorandums and counsels. In any society and in any government, there are research institutes, social science and political science groups whose opinions are well heard. We can operate through them.

It's also worthwhile to pique the interest of TV directors. After all, this topic is very interesting. If several famous people take part in discussing it, then of course it will be interesting enough, and they will be able to allow themselves the liberty, from the standpoint of safety, to bring these ideas to the public judgment. It is necessary for experts, including economists, sociologists, and psychologists to show, each from his own point of view, what the society of the immediate future should look like.

Nature compels us to bring up the young generation. We are not talking about ourselves—adults—now, but about raising children.

Today, not one country has an intelligible program of upbringing. All the education systems, including UNESCO (and I am not just informed about this from hearsay) are in a sorry state. They don't have any ideology or concrete plans. They are ready to hear out anyone who has ideas in this area because they have none of their own.

If we begin to offer the idea of integral upbringing—and this is something that psychologists, sociologists, educators, and teachers are already talking about—we will demonstrate the need for this within the framework of discerning what the society of the future is. We are talking about the future with the hope that we have one, and this will happen only if we can overcome today's universal, manifold, systematic crisis, which has nothing but human egoism in it.

How can we begin to rise above it? How can we elevate man so he can connect with other people without closing himself off, so he knows how to have a family the right way, how to coexist with the spouse and the children, with neighbors and coworkers? We have to elicit society's insistent necessity to resolve this question.

I don't see any obstacles from the government, church, school, or family. No one can object to movement toward unity among people. At least there shouldn't be any apparent objections.

Thus, we have to start with the department of education.

SELF-EDUCATION FOR CHILDREN AND ADULTS

- In order to realize this method, there have to be deliberately prepared educators who understand integral upbringing. How should their preparation be arranged?

- We have to set up television courses for all age groups. These educators can be 10 year old boys and girls, their 40 year old parents, and even the grandfathers and grandmothers. Everyone will study.

For those who complete this TV course, which will take three months, for example, and who desire to keep studying, there will be an opportunity to become a professional educator. We invite them. They will come to us for a seminar where we will see how they have absorbed, internalized, and learned the basics, and most important—the spirit! We will feel to what extent they can interact with people, and particularly with children. Then we will give them a scholarship and start teaching them. And alongside the learning, they will come in contact with children and form groups.

Once children complete their studies in regular school (in this regard we do not change anything), they get together in an after-school program where they are enveloped by integral upbringing. There they hold debates and discussions, develop contacts, and resolve conflicts the right way.

On TV, there are courses given to these groups that are demonstrational studies, while they realize them in their groups. That is how the system of preparation starts to operate, the system of training and further development of this entire system.

Every person finds his own place there. We need a great number of educators, and there is concealed unemployment all over the country. Educators receive the average salary. The children are busy. And there are no great expenditures.

As a result, we involve children and a great number of the adult population in self-education and upbringing. This process is mutual. It transpires constantly, both inside the individual and in his connection with others.

I think we can expect to see serious results within a few months. Society will be revitalized and all the costs will pay for themselves. We can ask and demand the means for these reforms from wealthy people, who will simply be ashamed not to participate in this because what's at stake is the future of the country.

This government program on the backdrop of today's void in upbringing and education is a virtuous step. That is how it should be perceived. We don't have to convince anyone. There are numerous scientists, psychologists, sociologists, and political scientists who understand that this is the cure for the modern society.

PRACTICE, EXAMPLE, AND INTERACTION

– An employee of one educational center, where several thousands of children study, watched our programs and became very interested. Her question was, "Is it possible to already start introducing certain elements of this method to a regular school? Or is this a cohesive method that simply won't work piecemeal?"

– This method can also be applied in parts, in any form, and it doesn't matter in what sequence. I think that the broadcast has to be done from the television center where this method is being developed. Experienced groups of children and educators will be invited there who demonstrate—literally on themselves—all the possible methods of work: debates, explanations, court hearings, various games, and communication.

This will be interesting for children and will guarantee a reliable job for educators. Simultaneously, we can send them aids. There's no problem delivering our message to any place and getting immediate feedback. Everything has to be made interactive.

– What principle will we encourage teachers to realize once they already have a work area, children, and questions? What has to happen first and what should be delayed for now?

– It depends on the age of the children. There has to be a strict division by age. There is a method that is suitable for children literally starting with ages 3-6, then 6-9, then 9-12 or 13, and so on.

If we are working with the age groups of 3-6 or 6-9, there is no place for theory or extensive explanations, only practice. At this age children study this world by putting everything in their mouths, feeling it with their hands. That is how they derive their sensations. Their entire research of the world is sensual rather than verbal. But older kids should receive explanations and write things down.

After age 9 a child needs explanations parallel to actions, answering questions such as, "What did we do and why?" "We have just carried out several successive actions; what did we accomplish by them?" The system is immediately made clear, a person receives explanations, and becomes his own educator.

Children over 13 already need a strictly logical approach: from where, why, what is Nature, geography, and history. They must receive an explanation of our current state and why we are obligated to interconnect, why we can be connected either by bad bonds or good ones, what is most beneficial for us, and where do we have to arrive in the end.

And of course, when working with adults, the first thing they need is not games, but explanations, such as expanded talk-shows. And of course, it has to be done in a respectable manner.

UPBRINGING FOR JUVENILE DELINQUENTS

– We receive many requests from organizations that work with children whose behavior is aberrant and who were unable to fit into the structure, such as juvenile delinquents. These organizations say, "Come to us and do whatever you want," because they have given up completely and don't have any idea what to do. Should we begin a dialogue with them?

– First of all, these organizations are open to us and that makes them a good choice. Second, they have the opportunity to subsist instructors and educators. That means that we have to enter there, but first of all, to work on psychology.

The children who are there are not receptive to anything and are closed off in themselves. They have a specific norm of behavior that is rigidly fixed and does not allow them to hear anything. But they are ready to hear about themselves, "What drives me? Why is this driving me or someone else? Why is he that way?" And so on.

They have to be approached from the standpoint of general psychology. This is interesting. It lets a person reveal himself and the behavior of others, "Why is he aggressive? Why does he get into fights?" Videotape them from the side and start showing them who they are. This will jab them. They will see themselves from the side on a stroll and in a fight, and then the educators should start explaining to them what drives each of them and why each of them behaves that way.

This way you will catch their interest. They will start seeing themselves from the side and hearing about motives for their behaviors which they did not even suspect existed. This will tease them and make them alert.

And then you will be able to talk with them, "What are the dark forces inside a person that compel him to act that way? Is this him? Or is it Nature deliberately playing with him that way, as if it's sneering at them, making a monster out of them to spite everything? And like puppets, they have to move to its orders."

If we show them this, we will easily touch every one of them because this kind of child turns his nose up at everyone, including himself. Losing his own sense of worth is the most horrible thing that can happen in that kind of environment.

This means that if we can get through to them with this first jab at self-love, we will win them over and will be able to work with them. In other words, we have to bring them to a state where self-love is truly satisfied.

We have to reveal the fact that right now they are not free, that they operate under the influence of instincts, practically playing a role that is programmed inside of them and that they don't have anything of their own. But it is possible to act yourself out in a different way, and start working with changing roles—I am instead of you, you are instead of him, and so on.

When we teach them to act each other out and to "enter" one another, the children will start to understand each other better. From there on it's a direct path to having them look at one another, studying and understanding each other, and becoming included in one another. When a child plays the role of another person, he creates that person's model inside of him, and then he can somehow unite, connect, and understand the other person.

I think that correction facilities are ideal settings for upbringing because the children there are in a closed area. We just have to make sure that our approach is very well thought out. Also, we must be patient, especially in the beginning. But it will start working quickly. If we use videotaping and then psychological analyses, problematic children will be very receptive to this because their self-love is highly developed, so we will achieve great success in such places– I served in the Soviet army in the 80s, which was in many ways built like a prison. Externally there's one thing, but in practice there's something completely different. During the day there were patriotic discussions, and at night—abuse and extremely abominable forms of interaction.

The official discussions that took place during the day would irritate people even more, in fact, making them furious because there was a colossal gap between what happened at night and what was discussed during the day.

When we begin to apply our method, what will happen to this gap? And what should be done about the nightly brutality?

– When a person begins to play the role of another person besides his own role, he begins to see what drives him and loses the motivation to act the way he did before. He no longer has the energy for the same kind of actions. That's because he is not himself; there's something sitting inside of him that's making him move. He already loses his patience with his own self.

I am sure that this will have an immediate affect on children's behavior both in closed communities and in open societies.

A HEALING PROGRAM FOR SOCIETY

– Suppose we create the ideal environment in which a child forms, but later he has to become integrated in the larger society. The problem is that there is nothing to become integrated into. There is no society and the social institutions are destroyed. And children don't aspire anywhere because they see that there is nowhere for them to go.

By raising these children on the laws of Nature, should we create new social institutions as they grow, or will they have to become part of something amorphous and completely unclear?

– Now we aren't talking about society, but about children. Without destroying anything and without creating anything new, we have to deliver our system of upbringing to every person.

If we are talking about society, then we need a special government program that would come down to having every person receive an hour a day from his employer at his workplace to watch and participate in this kind of program during work. He would continue receiving the same salary, but would be obligated to study for an hour of that time.

We're talking about viewing TV programs at the workplace where people from one or several departments get together in a hall. We broadcast a specific program to them where they see a group that shows them an example of the right interaction and analysis of specific conflicting situations.

In every company there must be a preparatory educator who will begin working with these people after they have watched several programs like this. Everything is aimed at showing a person that unification above egoism is productive.

I think the entire collective will immediately feel the result, including the grateful employer who won't feel that he is wasting an hour a day to have his workers do this. However, this is no longer a school program, although it practically follows the same method. We show a person who he is, what drives him, how to rise above himself and become included in another, and how to come out of himself. This involves role-playing where by acting out different roles we see ourselves from aside.

I think we will see how people begin to understand and warmly accept this approach. This program was initially prepared for children. It revitalizes society, making it more consolidated and warm, lowering tension and crime. It is bound to be accepted with gratitude and welcomed by the government. If presented correctly, through distinguished, famous scientists and social activists, it cannot fail.

We don't have any other choice. If not now, then a few years down the line this will be much more necessary and in demand—but it's a shame to let the time go by!

We will see how beneficial this upbringing is for everyone and in everything that surrounds us. We have to demonstrate that all problems lie in man's attitude to himself and others—to his environment.

We understand that it is very easy to turn a society into a dictatorship, in which case it stops being a society altogether. Democratic societies in the world existed or exist with the presence of many reservations, laws, and limitations because man's nature is aimed at buying up everything, suppressing it, not giving anything to anyone, and sharing with others only to the extent they can please you or service you in some way. This is the law of egoism.

All of the so-called democracy is built on preventing one egoist from running wild. It's necessary for other people to participate in ruling over society. That is, it's necessary to create a circle of egoists. They can do practically anything, while others are allowed slightly less. We will give them something for their existence too, and will give even less to a wider and lower circle yet. That is to say, for the sake of self-preservation, a hierarchy is created in the egoistic society.

The world is controlled by individuals, a small group whose members know each other very well and own everything. Everyone else gets whatever falls into their lot. That is how it's organized from above.

But now we are reaching a state where these powerful circles also understand the finite nature of their existence. They might have an enormous amount of precious metals, stones, and cash, but this won't save them because without becoming an integral world, we will simply consume ourselves like cancer and will cease to exist. Therefore, I think there is an audience we can turn to and a goal we can reach.

EDUCATIONAL WORK IN SUMMER CAMPS

- An Intensive Course in Love and Friendship
- "Good Internet" for Adults
- My Friend Egoism
- The Ideal Is All of One's Free Time
- The Environment Works on Everyone
- Rotation Is Necessary
- Self Service for the Sake of Uniting
- Learning to Be Merciful to Nature
- Pick Up a Backpack and Go for a Hike
- Begin with Small Groups
- Learning from Artificial Obstacles
- Nocturnal Adventures
- "We" Is Most Important
- Communication with the Outside World and with the Parents
- "Uncooperative" Kids
- Sitting with Friends by the Bonfire
- Being Your Own Psychologist
- Boys and Girls

In our days, we used to go to "pioneer camps." In other places there are summer camps, boy and girl scout camps, and so on. They exist in your system as well, and you also have practical experience. Why do you need camps like that? What's the point of having them?

– The main value of children's camps is that youth or children are taught the right connections with one another. They internalize the concepts of mutual help and friendship.

AN INTENSIVE COURSE IN LOVE AND FRIENDSHIP

There are several thousand children of different ages in our international educational organization. We begin this work with children aged 3 and continue through age 18. This is a very wide span.

We know how important the age criterion is for the children's upbringing and communication with one another. Naturally, this is the first thing we take into consideration when we assemble children from different countries. We try to set up a truly integral camp.

We compose a program that includes many excursions, discussions, songs, and common meals with participating. The children prepare the food, set the tables, and clean up after them. They service themselves completely. They are together 24 hours a day with educators present as well. And they go through the method of unification in a very interesting way.

The most important thing is to let a child feel, "This is how you depend on others and how others depend on you. This is how you perceive the world, why you perceive it as you do, how your attitude toward others changes your perception of the world, and why it is that when you interact with others correctly, you suddenly feel safe, inspired, enthusiastic, and stronger."

We show children how to build the right interconnections. We give them the appropriate material about human psychology and about our negative qualities. In fact, we practically don't have any positive qualities. It is written, "A person's heart is evil from birth." That is, we are all born egoists. It's good for children to grasp this correctly, to see real expressions of their personalities, habits, and egoism in relation to each other, and that they are always trying to profit by interacting with others.

So how can we transcend our natural drive? How can we connect with others in order to feel that bestowal, rather than reception, is pleasant and easy? This requires tremendous will power.

But we have to show children that bestowing is very simple, easy, fascinating, and enthralling. This can be a wonderful adventure where we are all so drawn to one another that we rise above ourselves and feel as though we're flying.

Giving a child the sensation of a new type of communication is very important. It leaves an impression or "informational recording" in him.

If these recordings follow one another with great intensity, at the same time as children recognize their constant descents into egoism, resulting in a descent-ascent-descent sequence, then a child begins to be in control of himself and understand how he can rise to a level where he will always feel safe, in love and friendship, surrounded by good friends.

That is, we show a child the obvious benefit of this kind of communication and unity. The most important thing in this process is to teach him to quickly come out of himself and enter this communication. This is a small, psychological tension that later stops being tension. It becomes habit or second nature once a child does it a certain number of times. And then it becomes easy for him.

When children return home after such a camp, they can set up similar small communities and practice within them. Besides, they stay connected with each other virtually. In the system of our constant studies, they continually perfect their ascent above themselves and their unity.

They really begin to feel something special in this unity, a different psychological state, comfort, and a life that's special, unbounded by anything, and not confined to narrow boundaries.

"GOOD INTERNET" FOR ADULTS

We hope that in time we will be able to present the same method to adults as well so they will also be able to experience the state of emotional comfort and will realize that a person's life can be completely different. There are many psychological exercises that enable people to start looking at life, society, and themselves differently, to see different possibilities of living and to be thankful for being alive. Then they won't be depressed, like half of humanity, and won't constantly feel dejected, stressed, anxious, protective, and on the defensive. This is what we are increasingly observing in our society.

Among adults we hope to do this through "good TV" or "good internet." We have an internet section called "a good environment." And we hope to attract people who feel bad or find life difficult and burdensome, with diverse programs, discussions, and productions.

A person wants to take his mind off things, but it's impossible to do that today. He turns on any TV channel just to see violence, problems, horrors, and constant struggles. In short, he sees vicious expressions of egoism and individualism. As a result, he is infused with these mindsets.

We think that if we let people see something else, they will gradually move away from these sinister examples provided for them by the mass media.

MY FRIEND EGOISM

– There are already events like this for adults, such as psychotherapists getting together for summer courses. To facilitate it, we have to determine several things for it to work properly. Does a camp have to be a summer event, or can it be done several times through the year?

– We are trying to organize these kinds of meetings any chance we get, whenever children have free time, such as during the second half of the day, on weekends, or during vacations. Besides, they can communicate with each other online and constantly be in these "good communities" from home.

It's very interesting to observe the times when they fall out of these communities. One minute they seem to be in a state of "We're friends, we're together, we are permeated by a common spirit, and everything is good." And suddenly, a few minutes later, you see how egoism breaks out and literally out of nowhere, without any apparent reason, they begin to compete and skirmishes arise between them.

This is a wonderful motive to figure things out and train them to stop and think. And it's not just to restrain the aggression, but also to remember the good state they were in where they treated each other differently, and to let that motivate them to achieve a higher state now by changing their egoism into a good connection, into friendship.

And suddenly the children begin to understand that this egoism is their friend, their buddy. It is always egging them on, pushing them toward each other from behind, and making them collide with each other, but in reality it is necessary in order for them to rise above it in a great connection.

Children begin to constantly guess what nature's plan is. They begin to understand that their own nature is egoistic and its constant agitation—a person's constant aspiration to subjugate another, to rule over another and to use him—is really a blessing, driving us to constantly develop altruistically.

Nature's profound plan is to turn us into independent people, yet in a constantly developing connection with each other. Then we will sense that we are constantly rising above our world. Thus, we begin to perceive ourselves as integral, feeling completely new spheres of Nature, its higher forces and integral plans. This is something new that cannot be present in an individualist.

There is a system in which individualists work, each of whom feels all the states only inside himself. But if we create the integral connection between us, we will feel the *entire* system, all of the information and forces that circulate inside that system. And then we won't feel bound by the individual sensation of our bodies, thoughts, and desires. We will come out to the next level of feeling life, which is called "human."

At first Adam was created, and then he "divided" into many people. This is how the Bible allegorically describes it. Therefore, we can call our common unity "Adam," and our common sensation is a certain basic sensation of Nature, which greatly differs from our individual perception of reality.

A person comes out of his personal boundaries and feels himself connected to the infinite, eternal nature, the eternal flow of energy and information. This gives him such an illumination in life that for its sake he is ready to accept any egoistic urges and overcome them.

THE IDEAL IS ALL OF ONE'S FREE TIME

– For this system to be adopted by the masses, we can use the internet. But it would also be interesting to find ways for the people who constantly communicate over the internet to meet physically. These camps can be a place where children from all over the world, who already communicate over the internet, could get together and meet in real life. How long should these gatherings be, a week, two weeks, a month, or perhaps the whole summer?

– It depends on the circumstances, but in principle, the longer the better.

That's because this is not the type of cure where someone gets treated and released. It is not a vacation where a person goes to relax and then returns home. And this is not study that is limited by a specific amount of hours.

Rather, it is non-stop communication where a person masters the method of creating a new, integral society. And children simply absorb it. It remains in them and can always be activated, renewed, and supported.

Therefore, the ideal is to do this on all of their free time. If possible, a child should constantly be immersed in this environment.

Imagine the following good fantasy: If we could take all the children in the world and create conditions for them where they would communicate with educators only in this environment.

THE ENVIRONMENT WORKS ON EVERYONE

– Should there be permanently operating centers so children could come there, leave, and return? And should the groups that get together there be small or large?

– It is easier to manage small groups in order to teach them the method, put them in the right kind of communication with one another, for them to hold dialogues, debates, research, analyses, and "court hearings" where they judge themselves and others.

This is tremendous inner, psychological work that a young person has to perform, and it requires certain conditions. Naturally, this work has to be interspersed with physical exercise, meals, trips, walks, and so on. That is, everything has to be coordinated. We have to give them time to let out the energy that builds up inside before we can sit them down to discuss something.

This can be done outside, in Nature, during a walk in the woods, in a park, or anywhere really. Say they went to the zoo, or to a river and something happened between them—they should immediately sit down and discuss it.

And we inconspicuously videotape ourselves from afar. When we observe something special, the person recording immediately makes a note to himself. Later we will watch this part of the recording and discuss what happened, how, and why.

In this process every person rises above himself, explains why this happened inside of him, and tries to assess everything absolutely objectively, with our help. Also, every person plays various roles. All of this has to be interspersed with various kitchen or cleaning duties.

During this period we show the children that a person should try to never leave this new attitude toward others. The most important thing is the fact that this does not consider just every person's individual work inside of him. We build the environment in a way that it influences *every* person and compels everyone to change. A person simply starts to feel the environment through his skin, as if he is in some kind of sphere that envelops him from all sides.

He feels the density of this environment around him and senses how everyone influences him, not allowing him to be different. That is, he is constantly held by others in a state of a good attitude to everyone, in a state of bestowal and love. They help him to instantaneously understand his inner egoistic urges and show him how to work with them.

A child sees his environment as a good force that constantly supports him like a kind mother and protects him from the inner enemy—egoism. A child has to receive precisely this sensation.

He starts to feel himself in the middle, between his egoism and the external environment. And then, like a judge, he comes to a state where he constantly decides whose side he wants to take. At every moment, he starts to feel how the opportunity of free choice, free will, emerges in him.

This is the point that nurtures the *human* within us, where the constant growth of egoism and the constant influence of the environment allow us to analyze and constantly choose which way to lean, with what to connect, and if we want to associate ourselves with our egoism or to embrace society, against egoism.

ROTATION IS NECESSARY

Say we create this kind of camp and we have children of different ages who are ready to take part in it, and who are already imbued with this method of integral upbringing. There are many organizational questions: Should the groups of children be fixed? Meaning, should a child be in one group for the entire camp or can we mingle them?

– Definitely mingle them. It doesn't even matter whom a child knows or doesn't know by name because we are getting them accustomed to the integral worldwide society, so they shouldn't care what someone's name is. I don't even care about his personality, thoughts, or feelings. All I know is that his attitude toward me is the same as mine toward him. We are trying to unite, to rise above our egoism and treat each other kindly. But how he handles himself on the inside and what he feels while doing that, how he struggles with his own self is his personal business.

I simply have to help him. I must deliberately show him my good attitude. That way I help him overcome the egoistic outbursts within him and rise above them toward me with the same kindness and friendsh– How do children of different ages interact with one another in this kind of camp?

– This is difficult. Even though they are learning the same method, they still have different attitudes toward the world, a different understanding of life, and inner makeup. Therefore, groups cannot be made without consideration of age.

However, we can create different combinations of these groups. For example, we can bring a group of 10 to 15 ten year olds and five 15 year olds whom we permit and guide to be the organizers and educators for the younger kids. Then the younger children will naturally learn from them and will be proud of having this opportunity.

That is, we do not mix up the group. We simply use the fact that younger kids naturally learn from older ones and are very proud when the older kids pay attention to them.

SELF SERVICE FOR THE SAKE OF UNITING

– How comfortable should this kind of place be? Should it be like a five star hotel or a tent in an open field? And accordingly, should there be self-service there?

– Of course, it's best to have as much self-service as possible, as long as the time is not used only on servicing ourselves.

If we choose an "open field" and put up tents there, then our entire time will be spent just on settling-in. Therefore, everything has to be prepared, planned out, and carried out, but with the children's participation.

We have to take part in servicing ourselves in a way where this activity serves as a basis for uniting, giving us the opportunity to work together. Our goal has to justify all of the work.

If peeling potatoes takes up the time we need to study, then things should be arranged so that someone else will peel the potatoes. But if we arrange things so that peeling potatoes becomes a joint activity of unification and an interesting study, then of course we will use it. Any work we do must be defined by how beneficial it is for upbringing.

– Can we introduce activities of labor? For example, we can arrange for the children to do agricultural work in the fields for several hours, which might be the first time they do something like that in their lives?

– Of course. Why not? Most important, any work should be sensed as common, so everyone sees that the success depends on each person individually and on everyone together, on supporting each other. This is necessary. It's possible to work at an assembly line where the result depends on everyone. It's worthwhile to think about which jobs to organize for them.

LEARNING TO BE MERCIFUL TO NATURE

– When people go to the countryside, they come into closer contact with Nature. In that case should they wake up at dawn and go to sleep at sundown? How can we use these opportunities of enhance man's interaction with Nature?

– The most important thing is to teach them a loving, merciful attitude to Nature. It is very important for them to feel the still, vegetative, animate levels of Nature and themselves as one, single whole.

A person can use everything from the lower levels of Nature (vegetative and animate) precisely to the extent that he requires it for life, but no more than that. That is how we come into balance and harmony, and begin to feel Nature as transparent, passing through us.

We feel it deeply and through it we feel its entire single force, the plan that has developed us over millions of years and is developing us still, leading us along. We begin to understand what happens to us if we merge with Nature. Yet, this union does not occur on the primitive level, but precisely through our unification with, and merciful attitude toward Nature, our love for it.

- So when we sit in a field or in a forest, we still talk about unification on the human level? The priority is always given to communication between people, while Nature is just a backdrop?

- Yes. But we discuss how and to what extent a person can use and exploit Nature, and what boundaries Nature sets up before us. Animals eat each other, and we too consume animals and plants for food. At which point is this consumption balanced and at which point is it considered excessive? We must define these boundaries strictly, and they must be instilled in our sensations.

That is how we train a child to be a member of the new society—the society of intelligent consumption—which we must come to now because we are exhausting the planet's resources.

PICK UP A BACKPACK AND GO FOR A HIKE

- Is there any point in organizing hikes and trips of various difficulty levels, such as a bicycle trip, a hike on foot, or a trip on a rowboat? These can all be used as challenges that allow unification to be expressed in action rather than verbally.

- Yes, of course. In these conditions we want to show them expressions of mutual help and interaction. We can also take girls along, in which case instincts and drives are bound to surface and all sorts of relationships will emerge, which won't be viewed above egoism, but inside of it. But they have to become convinced themselves of how much they are in control of themselves and how much they are not, in order to create a common male assistance to the women's group so they would express themselves as men. This is useful.

- From what age should these hikes and trips be arranged?

- Starting with age 11 or 12, no earlier. And starting with age 13 or 14, the trips could be done in mixed groups.

- Is it best to be in one place or to travel to a new place every two or three days?

- We can change places many times. But if we conduct great, intensive inner work, then they won't really notice the change of setting because the setting will be felt more internally—how they are closer together or farther away from one another. They will be focused more on their feelings and relationships.

Changing one field for another, or a wooden cabin for a tent, will be noticed less, like external, irrelevant conditions. If there is an opportunity to be by the ocean or a river, then in a forest, and then in the mountains or a desert, then there is a great difference between these places. And it will affect their interactions as well. But if it's just a change of place, that won't matter.

BEGIN WITH SMALL GROUPS

- There are several types of camps—huge camps, with thousands of children, or small, local, summer or winter camps. Which is better? Which is more suitable for the integral principle?

- It depends on the level of the kids' preparation. I don't think we should go for anything big in the beginning. We need small groups where everyone understands the goal we want to achieve.

Besides the educators, it is necessary to prepare the staff that will service the place. These people have to go through excellent training so they behave correctly with one another and understand what the setting and spirit in this camp has to be like. It is a place where a child becomes immersed in a completely different setting for perhaps several months, and even before that, prior to the trip, he is taught to be connected to others by creating the right virtual community, whose members support and help one another.

This does not require big children's camps. We have to progress with small groups, small communities that will become fully ready to assemble into a large community, while not losing the right orientation toward everyone. But we have to start with small groups.

– Should children who come to this kind of camp be prepared ahead or can they go through a "crash preparation" on the premises? Or, can the camp itself be a preparation for further activity?

– It depends on how long the camp will be. If you accept a child for two or three months, then you can accept anyone. For example, suppose there are 50 children. These 50 children are divided into five groups that sometimes work like five groups and sometimes merge together. But many parameters must be taken into account: Are the children similar in age, social origin, and mentality? If they match according to their external, domestic parameters, then in two or three months you will be able to turn any child into something new. In this case, you can accept any child.

However, it's preferable to have a backbone. Besides the educators, it's good to have children who are already prepared. It's like yeast that will provide a completely different formation, a product of the right fermentation, which will eventually have the necessary consistency.

It's necessary to have two teachers for every 10 children, and it's necessary to have at least one "senior" group among these 50 children, meaning children who are already prepared. Then there will be no problem accepting any children there. The "seniors" will quickly set all the others in order.

LEARNING FROM ARTIFICIAL OBSTACLES

– You said that a child's temporary space must be well organized. What's the best way to do that?

– The workday or school day has to be organized so the element of upbringing is present everywhere, in every activity, and in the daily routine. For example, arrange things so there is just one washing point and see whether they will fight over it or not. And start raising them right there and then. Or set up a very narrow place for food distribution or an insufficient amount of chairs, and look at how they behave.

They have to be placed in a position where they unwillingly have to adapt to your method and immerse themselves in new types of relationships. Otherwise they won't be able to stand it.

A child has to feel comfortable in any uncomfortable circumstance precisely because he rises above his egoism and treats others differently.

There are many opportunities to use deliberately placed obstacles to give them a hint that at every obstacle, at the barrier that is in front of them, they have to lift themselves to the human level and then everything will look different.

And many barriers of this type have to be created during the day, such as in games and on trips where they can't manage without one another. Maybe they will have to lie down one under another because that's the only way they will be able to overcome some obstacle.

This is well developed in the army and it's a worthwhile concept to borrow from the military. Suddenly someone might need to be carried on a stretcher or obstacles might arise where one person has to lie down and everyone else runs over him.

Special obstacles have to be selected and placed on every corner and at every turn. They can be physical or moral, and their objective is to constantly make the children collide with each other and then raise themselves higher. It's a constant training session.

NOCTURNAL ADVENTURES

– The next question I have is about nighttime. We know that half of all adventures in places like this happen after "lights out." How can this be arranged? After all, it's impossible to force them to go to sleep. Or should there be no lights out?

– Well of course things have to be organized, and very clearly. There has to be a lights out, but the children have to be made thoroughly exhausted, especially before going to sleep, so they are really tired and take pleasure in sleep and rest. But if someone can't fall asleep and everyone else is sleeping, then he has no right to bother them. He has to get up quietly and have a special room he could go to where "night owls" like him get together. They can sit there, talk, or watch our program on the TV or computer. And this is the only thing available. But afterwards we have to see what happens to them during the day?

So in this regard we also allow them to "let out steam" and avoid "taming" them into routine, letting them have an hour or so to themselves in the evening, like they do at home.

– With regard to the room where they sleep, is it better for it to be a big room for 10 children, or to have 2 to 4 kids to a room?

– It's better when the whole group sleeps together and the educators are nearby as well, at a slight distance. For example, the door to where the children sleep is open and the educators sleep nearby. There are 2 educators and 10 children who have an apartment or a house where they are all together.

Again, all of this gets mixed around, including the children who are in the group and the educators. They have to stop seeing each other. This is very important. There shouldn't be a scenario where one feels, "This is my friend." What about the others? Aren't they his friends, too? In other words, it doesn't matter who is next to me because everyone are my friends.

"WE" IS MOST IMPORTANT

– How should this reshuffling occur? Can it happen as a game or a lottery?

– It should happen arbitrarily and constantly. It can be done through a lottery or with a computer by random selection like in a slot machine. We can throw out selections of ten people per group using a meter of random numbers.

The children should understand that it doesn't matter who is in their group. On the contrary, the more unexpected and strange the person who ends up next to me, the greater my opportunity to attune myself differently through him, to sense things differently, and to ascend.

– What if the child doesn't want to change the surrounding environment?

– It will change anyway. What can he do about it? The machine gave out the results, and now these ten people are being replaced with ten others, and then with another ten, so there will never be repetition.

But if there is a certain period when some specific training is held, such as if something happened yesterday and today you want to discern something about it, then of course it's necessary to keep the same group. But a few days later the group still has to be changed. It's best to change the groups around as often as possible, and that includes the educators. A child has to feel comfortable in any society and to be able to connect with it. And everyone must influence every person correctly.

– But children don't always match one another in their qualities. Besides, even if we mingle them, they will still spend their free time with the people who are closest to them. How should we relate to that?

– Of course, we shouldn't intervene because they are drawn to one another according to their hobbies or because they came from the same place. They are children after all.

But this requires a creative approach from the educators. We have to show the children that ideally, you have to have an absolutely equal attitude to everyone. The world is built in such a way that we have to reach the level of total balance with everyone.

Of course, we are still far from this ideal, but we have to lead them toward it. It's clear that this specific person is your friend and you hang out with him in your free time. The two of you help each other and want to be together, sleep next to each other, go on a trip in the same group, and so on. But at the same time, we should help them detach from one another in some way.

To an extent, a person has to be like an individualist, feeling that he is not attached to anyone. He is attached to society, but to no one in particular. This is very important because one can eclipse the other. "We" is the most important thing. Not me, and not me with my buddy. "We" are just we, a certain common superstructure over all of humanity. In principle, it is faceless. This is one common image of man.

– What you just said fundamentally differs from psychology's approach.

– Psychology is built on encouraging a person, on giving him the egoistic energy to change within. It tells him, "Love your city, care about keeping your street clean... Love what's yours and yourself, and respect what's mine" meaning, "Try to play along with egoism." In this way, psychologists try to bring a person to something more social rather than individualistic. But that won't help. Our objective is the opposite: We have to lift a person upwards entirely.

– Should children have free time? And if yes, what for?

– Children don't need free time. They don't need anything. On the contrary, they are always playing games and being connected with one other. If you leave a child alone, what would he do? He will still play with someone.

– Yes, I remember how bored I was during my free time. I had nothing to do.

– Of course. It's horrible. What are you going to do—walk in the woods in some camp? There is absolutely nothing to do. A child shouldn't have free time, nor does he want it. A child should always be playing.

COMMUNICATION WITH THE OUTSIDE WORLD AND WITH THE PARENTS

– How does the communication with the outside world and with parents occur? It is very important to immerse a child into this special environment so he would be there for a long period of time. But should he still have an external connection through the internet or telephone? Can he connect to his relatives and the people close to him?

– Children can see, hear, and talk to their parents every day on Skype. The camp should definitely offer them this possibility. If the camp is somewhere out in the field, they can still go to some place where every person has the chance to talk to his parents for five minutes, but not longer than that. As for connecting with other, egoistic, uncorrected societies, this is absolutely unnecessary at this point.

We have to understand that if we are creating a new society, preparing a new human being, then he has to look ahead and never back. After all, children don't want to listen to their parents. They want to do everything their way and advance forward, while the parents stand behind them.

Parents should only give children the right setting and the right direction, and do everything they can so the children can advance. They should never try to pull the children into their own world. On the contrary, they should create new conditions for them so the children are only in them, and from there on, would move forward.

That is why we have to rear the parents ahead of time, before this small person returns to his family, by giving them an explanation of how they should express themselves in relation to their children. We are not trying to re-educate them. This is a completely different task that can only be done through the mass media.

But they can provide the correct routine for the children and support them every day, and to have the same routine be present at school, meaning, in their children's world as a whole. This is what we have to provide.

– What if the parents want to see their children physically, especially if the camp is intended for a long period of time? Should we organize parents' days?

– Yes, this can be done. Naturally, they won't have to see their children "through the fence." It has to happen handsomely and pleasantly. For example, we can hold a picnic together where children both perform and are also just next to their parents.

A child wants to snuggle up to his mom and to sit next to her, and she wants to see her darling child. All of this is obvious and natural, and we certainly don't prohibit any of that.

But nevertheless, this still calls for a briefing for the parents. For example, they shouldn't cry over their darling Johnny, "Oh no! He got sunburned or scratched..."

Parents have to treat the children with encouragement and even admiration because the children are in such a special camp. This is very important for the children.

– And how often should a "parents day" be held?

– I don't think it has to be done often. Maybe once every two weeks, and certainly not for the whole day. And during these days the children should carry out practically the same work as on regular days, while the parents can be together with them and observe how all of it is done from the side, including the games, discussions, courts, songs and dancing, and meals. And a couple of times a day they should be given half an hour or an hour of free time. It's necessary to show parents what this is.

This is how we also teach the parents to understand what is happening with their child later on. We have to organize these days in such a way that they will be educational days for the parents. When their child returns home, they will be able to understand how they should relate to various things and what "product" they have received after two or three months of camp.

The child is a completely different person, having a different outlook on the world and on life. The parents have to be ready for this. Therefore, during these days there should be very intensive studies for the parenWe have to give every parent a brochure and a CD that they will have to watch in preparation for the next visit. In general, this is mutual, intensive work that gives us the opportunity to literally perform a reconstruction of society around these types of camps. And not only parents can come there, but also grandmothers, grandfathers, and other relatives.

– Can parents work at the camp, or is it preferable for the staff to be strangers who don't have any familial connection?

– I think that in the future we will be able to create some kind of a resort for parents and children, where both children and parents participate in training sessions and go through mutual, psychological re-preparation, developing a new attitude to society, to creating themselves and a new community among them.

But this is already the next step. I can only envision it slightly, but it is premature to discuss it today.

"UNCOOPERATIVE" KIDS

– How strict should the discipline be?

– Everything has to be put on the table for discussion! We even have to seek out reasons for discussions with everyone afterwards. But it has to be a discussion, not a condemnation! In these discussions every child puts himself in the other's position—one time he is the accused, another time, the accuser, once he defends others, and then he defends himself, and so on. That is, we should help a person to come out of himself. We are all fighting our nature, which is an alien, internal mechanism that we have to rise above and use in the opposite direction. This is what's important.

– To resolve conflicts, is there any point in creating a working committee of educators and instructors who get together in the evening, for example, to discuss the day that has passed and the difficulties that occurred? Or should everything be done together with the children?

– The educators should definitely get together and discuss things. But mainly, all of the work on upbringing, order, and regulation of all the inner relationships should be constantly incumbent on the children.

Practically speaking, by the end of our work in the camp, the children should conduct all of their work, and be able to work on themselves independently.

– Sometimes a child destroys the space around him and doesn't fit in. In fact, he interferes with the processes. Under what conditions should he be expelled?

– There are several possibilities. If the child is difficult and doesn't understand anything because he simply doesn't hear it, that's not his fault. That's the way he is and you need to attach an older child to him who can influence him correctly. This is the best thing.

No adult educator can do this. An adult is perceived by a child as "furniture," null. But a child who's 3 or 4 years older is everything to him, and we must use it. An older child can turn to this "uncooperative" child and ask him to help in the kitchen or in another duty. That way, he occupies him for some time, taking him out of the collective and working with him individually.

Maybe this "uncooperative" child likes sawing, shaving wood, or hammering nails. And through that he will gradually enter the general atmosphere. And then, under the influence of the older child, he will begin to understand and feel what is happening here. These kinds of opportunities should definitely be created.

Expelling a child from camp and sending him home is an extreme case. It's only possible to do that if it's not a child anymore, but a young adult who cannot readjust psychologically. There are people like that, but they are very rare.

– There is a stereotype that if a person doesn't fit in, kick him out and that's the end of it.

– Definitely not! We cannot do that. We always use older children and the older environment in relation to the younger ones as intensively as possible. This kind of child can even be transferred to an older group. "You're 12 and that's what you're like!? We'll transfer you to the 15 year olds and see how you will behave there." The older kids will quickly "set him straight" and he will take on the right form.

– How should we arrange the interaction between the children in this environment, in the camp, and the "wild," local kids?

– We don't have local kids or "wild" kids. We must clearly select and know what we are doing. We receive the raw material of children, and we have to send them out as humans.

– But suppose we take a trip to some place that has local populated points.

– There shouldn't be any populated points. There has to be total isolation.

SITTING WITH FRIENDS BY THE BONFIRE
– Should there be flag raising in the morning and anthems at the end of the day? Should there be uniforms, and so on?

– We should have our own flag at these places, but no uniform. Maybe there can be special hats or T-shirts, but they don't even have to be identical. Maybe every group can have its own. But this is not necessary because the groups will be shuffled anyway.

However, we should have a banner of the future humanity, or something of that type. It shouldn't be done out of pride, as if to say, "Here we are, against everyone else." That kind of sentiment should definitely not be there. On the contrary, we are turned toward everyone with a bright face and an open heart.

The word "We" has to be written on the banner. And "We" is not ours or yours; it's everyone together, the common humanity.

- Should the day start with everyone gathering to raise a flag, and music?

- I think this would be good. The children should have a chance to feel proud, to be reminded of their great mission.

- Can we invite adult musical groups to these camps?

- What for? We will create musical ensembles right there, on the spot. Children have to have guitar lessons. They will all be happy to learn this. We should never have people from outside come there. Over three months we will create wonderful musical groups. This tremendously helps people to express themselves. Let them beat on the drums as much as they want there.

- Should we celebrate holidays there? And if yes, what should we celebrate?

- We have to celebrate our own holidays. Say we went on a hike. After the hike we perform, have a festive meal, give out ice-cream and sweets. And this is a holiday for us. It can include songs and maybe a bonfire.

There shouldn't be any general national or folk holidays. At least it shouldn't be done in a prominent, flashy way. This distracts everyone.

The most important thing is the integral society.

- You mentioned bonfires. Can you explain the significance of this phenomenon of people getting together around a fire?

- It's an ancient human drive. A person cannot tear himself away from a fire, from looking at the fire and feeling its warmth. Sometime we have to use these opportunities. But in principle, this should be done in order for the children to plan and direct this evening by themselves ahead of time, including their own songs or songs that were written by our friends previously, specifically for these types of gatherings. In principle, it's a gathering of friends around a bonfire. But it can also happen without the bonfire.

– When people sit around a bonfire, sometimes a very warm atmosphere, a special setting is created. Can we use that?

– Yes, but I think that people won't particularly feel the difference whether it happens by a bonfire or elsewhere. I think these children will begin to have such a feeling of togetherness that it won't depend on external conditions.

BEING YOUR OWN PSYCHOLOGIST

– Should we conclude events by drawing some kind of conclusions or presenting some kind of product such as a movie, or is it simply a process, so we come out of this event and enter a new process?

– This is a process that we go through daily. We select the most precious moments, the ones that are most useful for greater awareness, and make a movie out of them. The movie can even be several hours long because we were there for several months.

We collect all sorts of amusing incidents, special moments, their resolutions, and so on, and every person goes home with this movie.

Besides, every child should keep a diary. We give out special diary books to everyone and every child has to write in it every day. It should contain specific graphs: my attitude, their attitude, I am this way and they are different, something special that happened, how to solve a given situation, and so on. That is, a person must conduct psychological self-monitoring, and he must record it daily. After all, we are studying human nature.

The idea is that what they write will be read out to everyone. But that should happen gradually, not right away. We are becoming psychologists. We are working on self-attainment, and the diary has to reflect that.

A person has to come out of this process with a deeper understanding of who is sitting inside of him, how he should relate to the world—from the perspective of the little animal that's inside of me or from the viewpoint of the person I want to nurture within?

The writing should be done literally every day and be one to two pages long. It should include paragraphs marked ahead of time that describe specific things.

– Should a child fill out this diary throughout the day, or at the end, before going to sleep?

– I don't think it should be done before going to sleep. With children, everything changes very quickly. They are under such explosive inner impressions that we cannot expect them to accumulate all of it until the end of the day and only then to let it out on paper. We have to give them the opportunity to write in it little by little.

– How intense should these events be? Sometimes it's necessary to pause in order to really feel something. How packed should the day be with activities?

– It depends on the extent to which the environment excites us. A pause might be necessary, or more precisely, a change in activity. And it's possible that some of the groups might need a daytime nap, or some kind of breather, for example, to simply sit down to watch some kind of program, to do a calmer type of activity.

But in principle, I think everything depends only on the environment. Children can digest enormous amounts of information, absorb it, and adapt to anything. They don't grow tired of it. A child can play 24 hours a day. Everything has to be built in the form of a game. Then he won't get tired. He will only have to alternate these games.

BOYS AND GIRLS

– Should we have separate camps for boys and for girls or should they be in one camp? Or, should we take the boys to one place for a month and girls to another place?

– I think the last option is the best. In principle, unity can only happen among men. Things happen differently among women. The two genders unite on a completely different basis.

– What is the fundamental difference between these two forms of organizing a space?

– Everything we talk about is generally intended for boys. There has to be a special approach to girls and a special method that has to be discussed separately. This is not simple.

The sensation of yourself and the collective, unity, connection, "we" instead of "me" is completely different for girls, who are little women. And we have to develop a completely different approach for them.

One way or another, we are different, in fact, completely opposite in nature. Therefore, the organization of a camp for girls must be different. Generally speaking, creating a camp for girls is very problematic.

Men are drawn to one another. They want to be on one team, they need each other's help and a friend's shoulder. Their attraction to one another and to a group is instilled in them from childhood.

But women don't have this attraction. They cannot be connected with one another, other than through some kind of community that helps each of them arrange her life better. In that case they agree to something common. Therefore, here the approach must be different.

Their individuality remains. And it has to be expressed and supported, rather than suppressed. When working with boys, we aspire to make them view the collective as higher than the individual. We can't do that with women. We should not break Nature, but go along with it.

A woman helps men and pulls them closer to unity, while participating in this herself relatively passively, by transmitting to them her desire for a new society that will give her greater confidence and greater realization. But she does not personally participate in building it.

A man builds the new society, while a woman helps him. Without the female desire, a man will not do anything. The man is the builder; the woman is the force that directs him to build.

Right now the most important thing for us is to create the right type of men.

– Besides having a parents day, is it possible to organize a day when the boys prepare and girls visit, and they all have some kind of mutual activities?

– If both sides are prepared, then of course this can be done. But it depends on their age. Before age 11 or 12 there is no point having such meetings because neither of them needs it. Boys feel good alone, and girls feel good alone, as well.

Starting from about age 12 and up (in this regard, a lot depends on the social background and other factors), they start taking interest in one another. This even gets to the point where their entire lives, all of their time, all of their thoughts and desires are filled by the opposite sex. This is the period of swift hormonal growth. We have to understand it and take it into consideration.

Between ages 11 and 14 or even 15, we can organize mutual activities such as games, mutual discussions, and songs. They don't need anything more than that. This is an age when communication is mostly verbal, purely external.

At an older age they start having other types of communication, including sexual relations and everything else. If we imagine what the consequences might be, we have to decide whether or not we will allow them to be in contact with one another.

This depends on the society, its customs, and the mutual agreement of the parents so the organizers of these events don't have problems afterwards. This requires a very serious, thoughtful approach and preliminary agreement.

But we aren't thinking just about how to organize them together in their narrow, closed environment. We have to adapt them to life, so it's necessary to gradually (after a month of preparation) create a life-like environment, similar to the street, home, the playground, and school.

We have to practically lead them into real life, creating a setting that is as similar to the "battlefield" as possible.

It's similar to how spies are trained in conditions that resemble the places where they will do the real work. For example, in America, they probably build Siberian villages, and in the Moscow area they probably create something that resembles Manhattan.

So we should create the right conditions for them. And naturally, in these conditions, which resemble real life, there definitely have to be women.

INSTRUCTORS OF THE INTEGRAL UPBRINGING

- Theory and Practice for Educators
- Humanity's Lifesaver
- The Educator's Personal Qualities
- What Should Be Written in the Student Record and Why
- The Problem of Professional Fatigue
- The World Department of Education
- Educators' Master Class

THEORY AND PRACTICE FOR EDUCATORS

– How can educators become good specialists who create the right environment for the children?

– The preparation for educators has to be somewhat different than the preparation of regular school teachers because we are talking about upbringing rather than education. This requires expanded studies, which include the following topics:

- Children's psychology and group psychology
- Coexistence in an integral world
- The characteristics of the integral nature that is being revealed in our time
- Freedom of will and where it lies, the right to choose

- Man's egoistic and altruistic behavior
- The opportunity to shift from egoistic behavior to altruistic behavior under the influence of the social environment
- Creating a society that can change a person
- How a person changes under social influences, with the final goal of achieving a person's total integration in society

Educators have to go through a serious study of all these topics as a theoretical preparation for subsequent work with children.

They should also have two types of practical studies. First, the educators should hold discussions, debates, and discernments with one another, while we check how correctly they understand the basics of the new society.

Second, they have to imitate various states, "dress in" children's characters and each other's, and imagine their participation in the life of a children's group without making their presence stand out, thus preventing the children from acting naturally. They must develop the ability to guide children in the necessary vein of discussion, discernment, or analysis inconspicuously, like "secret agents."

This way, they can smoothly shift from the role of the children to the role of educators, acting out both of them. This will come in handy in their work.

And that's all. But this is not at all easy. First, it is necessary to find people with this ability. I am talking about men because the difficulties arise mainly with boys. There are fewer problems with girls, and for girls it's necessary to prepare female educators and instructors.

– In about two or three minutes, you have described practically everything that I have prepared on five pages.

– Let's consider this an introduction, a concise description of the basics. And now let's move on to the more detailed answers.

HUMANITY'S LIFESAVER

– There is a question about the prestige of the profession of educator. Currently it is not popular.

– When I was young I had a friend who was older than me and who had just finished school with the highest honors. By the laws of that time he could attend any academic institution, including the Moscow State University, without taking any exams. But he chose the local pedagogical institute.

Many years later I asked him, "What did you choose!? You could have gone anywhere you wanted! Physics, chemistry, biology—everything was open to you, any profession." It was enough for a simple lad from a provincial city to present his diploma with the highest honors on it, and he could already be a student of the Moscow State University! And he replied, "The profession of an educator was so honorable that I had no doubt about where to go to study since I had the chance to enter a pedagogical institute without any exams."

I was 7 or 8 years younger than him. Over these years the priorities had changed and teaching became a completely unappreciated profession! The people attending pedagogical departments were those who wanted to get a higher education but were afraid they wouldn't be accepted anywhere else. The only department worse than the pedagogical department was humanities. I remember this "honor" hierarchy.

But now we are facing a crisis that we can only come out of by rearing the new generation of educators. Today there is no person more important than an educator, but an educator (not a teacher), who understands the current and next state of humanity that we have to reach if we are to survive. He theoretically and practically builds the young generation and shows all of humanity the new, positive level. He is the modern-day savior.

Everything depends on the extent to which we can show, through mass media, that the crisis has only one solution. And only these people—the educators, are our lookouts, our leaders.

Great preliminary work will be required to explain this to a wide circle of the population. But I think that on the backdrop of the crisis in education and upbringing, the situation in families, and problems such as abundant drug abuse and depression, it won't be difficult to raise the importance of the right upbringing.

– For now, an educator or a teacher is unfortunately not a prestigious profession. And it's very rare to notice real men in children's establishments, men who are educated and strong, who have a real personality, who look like and are wholesome people. By the way, your center is different in this regard because the men working there are real, educated men. This is the first place like it that I have seen.

– How can it be any other way!? We entrust our children, the most precious thing we have, the future of the world, to these people! In 10 years these children will become adults and will take our place. Today we are forming the future world—our children and grandchildren. There is nothing more important to a person than to be sure that his children will continue the right path and will feel good, comfortable, and safe in their world!

Even animals choose their place of gathering, form their flocks, and build dens based solely on considerations of the safety of their offspring. To them, it is the most important thing. All research of the animal kingdom shows that their behavior is guided by care for the safety of the youngsters.

And what about us? Let's at least be on the level of animals! Of course, we will rise higher as well, but let's provide at least this level for now.

Yet in the meantime parents are forced to throw their children to the whim of fate, to place them in learning establishments where they don't know what is being done to them. Boys start to come out of women's influence only at age 18! And after that they go to the army [in Israel], where everything turns out completely opposite to their previous experience. They go through an enormous inner crisis, a shock. Life appears completely different because it starts being arranged in a male manner rather than a female one. And because they are not adapted to that, they are forced to break themselves.

We shouldn't raise Spartans, but we should prepare them for the right interaction with one another. Women cannot transmit this to men because their interaction is special, female, with each of them existing by herself. They can be imbued by some common movement, but while still remaining separate.

For men, movement forward happens only in cooperation, friendship, and unity. Therefore, boys are completely unprepared for the future state, in which they are integrally connected, comprising one, single humanity, "we" instead of "me." Women cannot prepare them for that!

It's necessary to have educated, strong, male educators who have a good understanding of the integral psychology, who know how to attune every child separately and all of them together toward cooperation, who can demonstrate every step of the way that we cannot achieve any goal without unity, that any solution can be achieved only through greater unity between us.

When a person faces any challenge, he should immediately have the right reaction to it. He should immediately think, "In order to solve it, I need to unite with others, and only in the unity with them will I find the right path."

– How can this situation be turned around so that well-bred men would nevertheless understand how important this work is and would start raising children?

– The crisis is developing and demonstrating to us the critical necessity of this profession.

There are seven billion people currently on the planet. Half of them are women, who will become female educators.

But of the other half of the population, the male one, about 30% are children. Everyone requires upbringing, but we are talking about children first and foremost. This means that 20 percent of the world population needing upbringing are children of different ages, up to age 18. It turns out that over a billion people are children. If we consider that there has to be one educator for every five children, then can you imagine how many educators we need!? About 300 million. And this is a profession requiring a good preparation and the right people, who need to be selected.

We are talking about unemployment, about the fact that we don't know what to do with the excessive population of the earth? Then reform all of this population, make consumption reasonable, without excess in one place and hunger in another. Find these 300 million educators, who have to become real reformers of the world. And then you will see a completely different layout of the entire human civilization! This is what we should aspire to.

Naturally, UNESCO, the UN, all of the international organizations and governments must take part in this process. All the resources should go toward restructuring interpersonal relationships and creating them on a completely different basis.

The most important thing is the preparation of the educators, the instructors who will raise the next generation. For the first time in history, we are working on building a human being, raising the human being in man.

A person is first and foremost an integral unit of society! Integral, not individual, which is what we currently consider the highest value.

The crisis is forcing us to rebuild all of society. Care about the future, about the doomed generation, will become the reason for humanity's correction. That is how children raise the parents, forcing them to change.

THE EDUCATOR'S PERSONAL QUALITIES

– Just like any other profession, the profession of an educator involves professional deformation. That is, any activity a person does changes him, distorts his personality, and tapers certain personality traits.

– Except this profession, since all the people in the world will have to become both their own educators and students of themselves. And each of them will have to position himself the same way in relation to others. A person rears society, the environment, and the environment consists of everyone, so everyone should be both a teacher and a child.

– For many centuries teachers received officer's titles. They walked around with weapons and other male attributes. Half of the educators in your organization are also former army officers. They are serious, athletic men.

– Many of them served in the army and some have high officer's titles.

– Is it appropriate to bring back masculinity to the male collective to differentiate men from women, to alter the "unisex" society that now exists?

- There shouldn't be any "unisex"! Boys have to feel like men, like the owners of the planet, preparing to truly possess it. And not only the planet, but the whole universe. This is necessary.

In our groups we study man's nature, his freedom of will, the opportunity to realize it, and a person's influence on the world. By studying it, we see that you cannot conquer Nature by force. Currently, man is doing nothing but mutilate it, creating an inhabitable environment for himself. So it's unlikely that children will respect strength in their educators and teachers.

Boys have a physical inclination for sports and games. This gives them a physical outlet to let off steam when needed. And there are educators who hold these sessions. But of course, they don't influence the children with their physical force.

- We said that educators have to alternate, and a boy has to be accustomed to expressions of completely different qualities in the educators. But on our part, we are insufficiently brought up and therefore, without noticing it, an educator automatically suppresses the children. What can we do so this won't happen?

- Everything has to be aimed at enabling the children to self-educate themselves, so they will organize themselves and hold their own discussions, and courts. The educator is like a "secret agent" in their midst, slightly guiding these processes.

But if the situation becomes heated and the children are unable to set things right on their own, then this is the only case when the educator can express himself as an organizer and educator, use his authority, and force them to get back to the correct state.

- How can we prevent the educator's authoritative influence from becoming a reason to fear him?

- The use of physical force is not even a topic for discussion! Children have to see that the educator intervenes only in order to put them back into the boundaries. And to achieve this, he can only use explanation.

In every group of 10 children, there must be 2 educators. And if any child becomes disobedient and interferes with everyone's studies, he should be influenced through the group and this has to happen immediately. Every child should constantly be formed through the group. That is the only way it should happen.

Of course, this is an art! But it's an enthralling art, which gives you the chance to see the fruits of your labor immediately.

It is expressed in children very quickly and remains in them naturally. They immediately adapt and then immediately forget because egoism constantly grows, especially during childhood. It explodes, as if nothing was created a minute ago, instantaneously erasing everything, and you see an egoist in front of you all over again. So where did everything go? It did not go anywhere. It's just that greater egoism has come to the surface now. It is constantly growing, and an educator must form it into an altruistic, integral attitude to everyone.

- You said that it's very important for an instructor to treat a child like an adult. But a child is not an adult.

- He shouldn't be treated like an adult, but as an independent, responsible person. However, this should be done without forcing or pressuring him. It has to happen on the level that a child has to behave according to his age.

- There is a difficulty here. On the one hand, I relate to his opinion seriously and respectfully, but at the same time, I always have to remember that he is still a child. Or is that wrong?

- Our entire life is a game. What does that mean for us? We have to show children how we relate to them and the kind of behavior we expect of them. Once we are convinced that they have understood and accepted our approach, that they have seen it, we ask them to show the same approach toward younger kids, which allows us to see how they have understood it. That is, we check whether they can "settle into" our character, understand us, and demonstrate this to the younger children. This should be done carefully and tenderly, unnoticeably straightening them.

Who are we raising in a child? An educator. When he knows what it means to be an educator of a younger child, he understands me better as his educator as well. Thus, we develop a relationship of equals. When I teach him, he understands why I am behaving this way and builds his behavior accordingly. A few days later, he will go to the younger group and display the same behavior.

Within every person, we are creating his "self," his juxtaposition with the higher level—the educator—and with the lower level, the students, in relation to which he is the educator. It turns out that every person is a student of the higher degree and an educator of the lower one.

The sensation that you are a link in this chain has to be natural for every one of them. This is the basis for society's integration, with each of its members suppressing himself both as a student and as an educator. This is studied as part of the basics of group interaction.

For the sake of attaining an integral society, I have to consciously lower myself before the environment, practically annulling myself before society. And on the other hand, I have to elevate myself in order to feel society's dependence on me, and affect it with the importance of the goal.

The lowest level and the highest level have to be realized in every person. And the difference between them determines a person's inner height.

– Should the educator also be on these two levels? Also, should he have a vividly expressed childish, playful part in him?

– Of course.

– Very often the people entering this profession had a problematic childhood and wish to compensate for it through the children.

– I understand. Often the people who become educators lack self-esteem. They go to a group of children in order to rescue themselves, to compensate for their lack of feeling of safety and confidence.

But in our upbringing we have to choose completely different people and form them! I would accept to this course anyone who wants to join. At the very least, a person will learn something and will move closer to the new, integral society. Something will penetrate him and he'll change. Afterwards, good instructors should be selected out of them, people who can play and position themselves well.

Instead of their "I," they have to have the importance of the goal. "We" has to occupy the most important place within them. This kind of person should not be afraid or ashamed of not having an "I." He is not like a rooster that wishes to rule over everyone. He is proud because his job is necessary for the collective, because we will find the truth and our new existence in our unity.

– There are several ways to determine the qualifications for people who work with people. I will name three of them.

1. One is tests. When a person passes them, he gets a diploma and may start working.

2. The second is when a community of educators determines that the person is suitable for it. The opinion that "he is one of us" is enough to consider him professionally qualified. That is how psychotherapists are accredited.

3. And the third way is when the children themselves decide whether this educator is suitable for them or not.

In your opinion, what should be the criteria to determine whether an instructor is ready for this job? What should make him qualified enough for people to entrust him with children?

– Every man has to be a father and every woman—a mother. Every person has to understand what is an integral society and how to interact within it, both with adults and with children. Therefore, everyone has to complete these courses, which should be opened everywhere.

All the mass media channels should talk about this constantly. It is necessary to free up every working person for a certain number of hours a day to study these courses.

If an adult who has completed studying these courses, and understands their importance, is drawn to working with children, he can be selected for learning how to be an educator. But even those who are not selected for it will become better parents and better members of society because they will understand the necessity of interaction among everyone.

During the study we notice the people among all of the students who are able and willing to be educators. The selection process here is very simple because there aren't many people wishing to be educators. Working with children is not easy. It requires patience, attention, and the ability to constantly be under pressure with children.

This is not a job, but a vocation! Only love and a sense of responsibility can give one the strength and the patience for it, and allow one to make this choice. It is where we create a new humanity.

I hope that there won't be problems with the work force. It's not difficult to tell whether a person is right for this type of work. Perhaps certain tests will have to be prepared. But I don't think they will be tests on paper or multiple-choice exams. Rather, the selection will happen in practice.

A great number of educators will be required for children and adults of all ages and of all levels of preparation. I think there will be work for a lot of people in this area. This can solve the unemployment problem that will be exacerbated all over the world as we cut back on the production of unnecessary products.

– Should we pay attention to the children's opinion about whether or not they like an instructor or educator?

– Yes. We have to pay attention to the children's reaction and together with them discuss why they like one educator or why they don't like another. The educators should also explain why they act the way they do. They shouldn't conceal the methods of their influence, have secrets, or secretly manipulate the children! Definitely not!

Educators and children go through the process together. We are creating a new society and are working together on our evil—our egoism, trying to give it the opposite quality of bestowal and love.

This does not and should not involve any secrets or manipulations. There shouldn't be any teacher's rooms where they hold closed-door conferences or short coffee breaks. On the contrary, we can discuss everything with children absolutely openly. This is a completely different approach to life!

We are facing nature's challenge. It created us as egoists and is placing a task before us—to change ourselves. This is our common problem! And to the extent that each of us feels that he is an active participant in solving it, instead of passively waiting for correction, to the extent that he independently forms himself and the environment, the process will be creative.

It will be important for everyone. Every person will feel his responsibility and won't be able to escape it. In this regard, children and adults are equal.

WHAT SHOULD BE WRITTEN IN THE STUDENT RECORD AND WHY

– You said that it's necessary to keep a record, a personal file for every student where information about him is kept. What information should it include and how open should it be to the child?

– I think there should be nothing secret in this file. The educators will record their observations in it, and the children will also have diaries where they will mark the phases of transformation from animal to human.

Even though we walk on two legs, we are still animals because we are completely subjugated by the force of Nature. However, by rising above our egoism and building an altruistic nature atop it, we rise above Nature and become people.

The "human" level does not exist in Nature. As a psychologist, you know this. Biologists and geneticists also confirm this. A human being is what we create *within* us. So the phases of the development of a human being in each of us are very interesting.

When I asked my teacher about this opportunity, he answered, "Yes, it's worthwhile to make concise records about your main findings within you. It will let you get to know yourself better. Later you will see what you went through." Today I can read this diary or look into my inner diary to see the phases I've been through.

Looking at my students, I see that they go through practically the same phases. Naturally, every person goes through them in his own style because we differ from one another in certain things. These records will be useful for self-analysis if every child studies himself in this way. But it's not for anything other than self-analysis.

Our progress forward is self-attainment and the attainment of the whole world through ourselves. By developing ourselves, we see the world as more developed, wider, and richer.

For an educator, the student record is the mirror of his work. He doesn't inspect the child through it, but checks himself, "Did I really act correctly? Is the child advancing along the right steps? Are there any vicious cycles that the child is constantly repeating?" That is, the student record is first and foremost a record about the educator.

– If the child is interested, can these records be one more reason to talk to the educator?

– Of course! We are all people and there is nothing secret here. The more open we are, the more we understand each other and have to know each other, and know that we simply must unite

PROFESSIONAL BURNOUT

– One very important problem is people "burning-out" professionally. Many people working with children and with adults "burn out" after a year or two. They simply can't bring themselves to go to work. One reason for it is that a person does not use his entire personality when interacting with children. He uses only a narrow part of it. When this happens, everything else within that person is not activated, eventually causing inability to keep doing the job.

You are saying that an educator has to be a person first of all. He has to have an "adult half" and a "child half." Is it possible that the educators will also "burn out" after a year or two? If so, how can we overcome this problem?

– You want to place your instructors in our educators' place, but it doesn't work.

– Yes, I see that.

– And it won't work. With us, the educator is the most important member of society. He lives the same life as the children's parents and grandparents, as the mass media, and as everything. He lives it! It is not some small part of him that might burn out because he cannot express himself. He participates in the most creative process in the world. All of life is connected to him, the children he raises, their parents, and all of society in general! We are forming a new generation, the next level, and I would even say—a new dimension into which humanity is entering.

We have to give it everything we have. We do not have a personal life, the private life of our family or ourselves, or our own friends. All aspects unite into one whole. There cannot be any fatigue or one-sidedness here because I am in this entirely. In this area, I have to realize my habits and interests, my relationships with my parents—even if I am an adult, with my children, with my family, and with the entire society around me I don't see this profession as being separate from the world. On the contrary, I am at its core. Together with all of humanity, I work on transforming myself, on bringing myself into balance with Nature, which is showing us the universal, integral interconnection of all of its parts. And I am forming this together with others.

We hold gatherings, conferences, and exchange experiences. Society lives all of it, so there is no place here for professional burnout! This is our *life*, and it continues the way it is.

However, if a person does suffer from professional burnout, he should be transferred, such as by giving him the chance to provide an upbringing and teach at corporations. Or he should be transferred to a different type of work, such as production. But I don't think this kind of problem can arise here.

THE WORLD DEPARTMENT OF EDUCATION

– Should people be able to enhance their professional knowledge by traveling to other countries to exchange experiences?

– I think it's necessary to create a Supreme Council of educators, similar to UNESCO or as part of UNESCO. It should have great authority and be highly respected. Its tasks will include developing methods and recommendations, maintaining contact with the whole world, and adapting the method of integral upbringing to different parts of society.

The current human society consists of seven or eight civilizations whose contact with one another is very negative and conflicting. We should create a method of upbringing for each of them that will smooth out their contact with the others, until they become completely included in one another. This is an enormous task that can only be carried out by a great number of specialists. But there has to be one brain center.

– What is that brain center? How is it structured?

– It will consist of people who understand what is happening in Nature and in the human society, and have the ability to unmistakably discern which qualities in us can be corrected using our freedom of will, which of our qualities we can actually change in order to become a harmonious part of Nature.

These people can feel what separates us from Nature— the conflicts, separation, and antagonism. They perceive our opposition to Nature very keenly and can therefore discern what we should change and how we can do it.

These people exist, and they have to be brought up. They will comprise the backbone of humanity's ministry of upbringing.

– A government of sages has always appealed to people. Throughout all of history people dreamed of a society that would be governed by sages.

You said that there are several civilizations and the conflicts between them can be smoothed out by upbringing. Can you give an example of at least two civilizations, and how you see their unification happening?

– Today there are conflicts between the European, American, South American, African, and Asian civilizations, the Asian one dividing into several: China, India, and the Arab countries.

This is an enormous gathering of civilizations that are coercively connected and intermingled, and which are in friction with one another. Unwillingly, we are connected by common technologies and are forced to be in contact with one another.

Previously, we were divided. Within each of these civilizations, egoism worked correctly, people understood each other, knew the conditions of a non-conflicting co-existence, and everything was normal. But today civilizations are starting to collide and to chafe against one another with sharp edges. For example, look at what's happening between the European civilization and Islam.

China is on the rise, being an obscure body that exists throughout the whole world in the form of hundreds of millions of immigrants from China. Just a few decades ago this was a completely closed country! But today it's the opposite. It is becoming open to everyone and is coming out to every country in the world.

The world is changing very quickly, while our upbringing is not keeping up with these changes. Nature is bringing us together, while we are reluctant to communicate with one another. This is particularly evident in Europe, which is being encroached by other civilizations. They live there in insulated islands, implanting their culture and wishing to live in their own way. But Europe cannot absorb them in this form, and as a result, frictions emerge. For now we are trying to smooth them out somehow, but it's an explosive situation. When it explodes, it will be an extremely powerful blast that will reverberate the world over because these improper mixtures exist everywhere.

– So you're saying that integral upbringing will make children of different civilizations similar to one another?

– There won't be any difference between them! We are doing this in our groups, and there is no difference between the children. But this kind of upbringing cannot be implanted by force. People have to *want* it.

Everything has to submit to the common "we," the unity, which Nature exemplifies for us. And there is no other option. Whoever is against it is an enemy of Nature (but not ours, mine, or your personal enemy). He simply does not have the right to continue to exist in this form; he has to change himself!

– We are currently exposing and offering this method to different civilizations. Will they accept it for their upbringing?

– We cannot go against Nature because we exist within it. We cannot invent our own laws if there are laws of gravity, preservation of energy, informatics, and so on.

It's necessary to clearly discern the laws of proper interpersonal interaction in the integral world. And if someone doesn't want to study and observe these laws, we won't accept such people into our system. Then they will realize that it's impossible to go against Nature, or they will simply see the kind of suffering and losses this leads to.

The future has to be integral. This is what we are discovering today.

– Will it be that obvious?

– You can find thousands of articles on Google, researches in any field of science, describing what our world is becoming. They all say that the world is round and integral, that all of its parts are interconnected and intermingled in one another, and that only humanity is egoistic, opposite from Nature. We will survive only if we set ourselves right by balancing ourselves with Nature.

These are not my personal theories. I read about it in hundreds of articles by serious scientists who research this problem from different sides and positions. They include representatives of different civilizations and they are not fanatics. They understand that we have to follow Nature instead of being stubborn and resisting it.

EDUCATORS' MASTER CLASS

– When you describe an educator's work with children, I see that it is very similar to how you work with your students. I understand that it is not pure theory, but on the contrary, an absolutely practical science. I only have one question: How can it be adapted and circulated as widely as possible? Could you hold a constant, perhaps virtual, master class for beginning groups?

– Of course. All the problems that emerge in the groups have to be video recorded. Then I can watch these videos and advise. I will also be happy to hold practical studies with adults and children.

When children learn to behave correctly and relate to each other in a good way, they work wonderfully in a group. But suddenly a breakdown occurs, an enormous outburst of egoism, and it doesn't happen to just one or two children, but to everyone simultaneously. It's as if some virus infects the whole group all at once. What should they do in such a case?

Immediately record it on video, research it, and show it to others! We are dealing with life, with matter that demands correction, fulfillment, and healing. I would like to participate in these critical, dramatic situations. This is interesting.

– Advanced educators who are already working with children have many questions. Would it be possible to organize practical master classes for them?

– Yes. For educators, practice is the most important. They receive the basics of the theory in the very beginning of the study, but later theory and practice have to occur simultaneously. That is, for several years, they should regularly get together for their own studies and discuss what happens in the groups they work with. This is necessary.

Of course, I can participate in this as well. I have to establish a return connection with them in order to know about what is happening in the children's groups.

I think we can hold lessons over the internet for our entire worldwide educational organization. This, in fact, is what we are doing. We send out all the materials, printouts, and videos. If this is not enough, we can hold interactive discussions where they ask questions and get answers.

– I think it will be clearer if you discuss specific situations that were filmed on video.

– Here's an example. A few days ago the senior instructor at our education center came to me and told me about a situation that happened in a class of children aged 10 to 11. Suddenly, out of nowhere, an enormous egoistic outburst occurred, instantly destroying the good relationships that had formed among the children.

He and I agreed to analyze this situation, discern the details to the maximum, discuss it with everyone, and then decide what to do. And this should definitely be done together with the children, rather than behind their backs!

It's possible that once we film these moments on video, we will show them to the children. Then we will ask them to change places so that each of them plays the role of his opponent and sees what is happening to him, what he looks like to someone else. Then we will ask him to play the role of the educator and ask him for advice about how we should act in this situation, effectively telling him, "Go ahead, solve this problem, we want to see how you cope with it. You are men, so do it."

You said that it's necessary to create a method of integral upbringing for literally everyone so everyone would rise to a common level. Is it possible for parents and grandparents to participate in this along with the children?

– As an example, let's take a family in which three generations live together: children, parents, and grandparents. They are connected with each other and with the rest of society because each of them connects with his peers. Discovering our interconnection through the connections within a family is very important and interesting.

THE ESSENCE OF INTEGRAL UPBRINGING

- At the Height of Egoism
- Humanity's Salvation Is in Studying the Laws of Nature
- The Law of Universal Interaction
- We Are Talking About Survival
- A Bunker Won't Save Us from the Integral "Tsunami"
- From "Me" to "We"
- The Necessity to Create a Global Organization
- No Discounts for Age
- The Language of Inner Contact
- Integral Ideas for the Creative Arts
- The Female Desire Will Correct Everything
- Let's Unite

– Can you explain what is integral upbringing and how it differs from what everyone commonly knows about education and upbringing?

AT THE HEIGHT OF EGOISM

– In our world, any object's similarity or proximity to the surrounding conditions is comfortable for that object. Nature aspires for balance with the environment in which an object develops (in terms of temperature, pressure, and various other parameters). The same thing can be said for the human society. We always adjust ourselves to the environment; it compels us to do so.

But we are less sensitive to Nature. We don't wish to be closer to it, preferring instead to surround ourselves with an artificial environment. We build houses, cool some things down and heat other things up, and create numerous artificial things.

A similar problem exists in society. We develop gradually, by formations. But today we have reached a new state where Nature, which forced us to come out of the caves, is forcing us to build an integral social life on the planet.

We have gone through all of the phases that were based on the development of egoism. The egoism constantly grew in us, compelling us to repeatedly transform ourselves and adjust to the environment.

Now our egoism has peaked. It seems to be losing its orientation, not having anywhere to keep developing. As a result, half of humanity is outright depressed, and probably even more are experiencing disguised depression. Additionally, there is international terrorism, abuse in families, economic problems, depletion of the earth's natural resources, hyperactivity in children, and so on.

We have reached a certain borderline that has been outlined by sociologists and other scientists. Doctors are noticing a drastic rise in the population's psychological instability.

In the last few decades, Nature has clearly manifested its integrality. Whether we want it or not, to survive and to exist more or less comfortably, individuals and society as a whole must study this new state. We are being "cloaked" from the outside by the entire surrounding environment, and we have to assume its form.

What is the meaning of humanity's "integral state"? It is the interconnection of all the people. We see that one way or another, all people end up being interconnected, but not by their own will. They resist it, while Nature compels them to it. That's why crises emerge, including problems in the political, economic, and government realms, and even between children and parents. Our unwillingness to become similar to Nature evokes ecological cataclysms and natural disasters that threaten us.

According to many researches, we have crossed the point of no return; there is no way back. Where are we going? What should we do?

HUMANITY'S SALVATION IS IN STUDYING THE LAWS OF NATURE

My first profession is bio-cybernetics, where I studied systems. In closed systems, an integral, analog system requires all of its parts to be in complete interaction with one another. The system can work efficiently only when its elements interact in a coordinated fashion.

When a system is affected by an outside element, oscillatory processes occur, which gradually bring it into balance. Once the system's balance is restored, it steadily reacts to the external influence.

Our task is to bring ourselves to this steady state while reacting to Nature's signals, which we receive on all the levels. In a closed system, external influences are met with resistance. The people who control this system usually balance out the external influence willfully. So what should we do with ourselves? How can we bring ourselves, our system of cogwheels that are locked together to correct, coordinated spinning?

This is humanity's whole problem. And we will have to solve it. Many specialists write about it very convincingly, but what's the answer?

In our research center we are working on this problem, trying to solve it theoretically and in part practically, in small experimental groups, including groups of children, adults, men, women, and mixed groups. We are trying to discern specific tendencies, possibilities for a solution, and shortcuts because humanity does not seem to have a lot of time left.

Work in an experimental group is very far from real life where we encounter people who don't want to know anything about the systematic approach, do not understand it, and object to it. But we will have to make contact with them somehow. It's like trying to explain to a seriously ill person that he needs treatment, that he shouldn't think he can go on living as before, or not think about anything at all, come what may.

We are trying to solve this problem, but in principle, it is the problem of the whole of humanity concerning its future, integral state.

Will we be able to solve this problem through upbringing? Suppose we have 10-20 years left. We will address society through the mass media, governments, UNESCO, and the UN.

We should orient ourselves by the current children, those who are about 5 years old today. We should work on raising the young generation that is under our influence. Considering that young people enter the circle of life at ages 15-20, we have 10-15 years to work with them.

During these 10-15 years, can we turn them into the people of the future generation, which is not that far into the future anymore because the natural factors are closing in on us and we are lagging behind?

It all depends on what system of upbringing, program, or method we will use to carry out our work, alongside preparing expert educators, attracting mass media, governments, and international organizations. For everything to start spinning in full force, everyone must recognize the urgency of this work. Then, in 10-15 years we will really have a new generation, adapted to the new conditions of Nature. This is the challenge that we must address in regard to the integral upbringing that we need to implement.

THE LAW OF UNIVERSAL INTERACTION

– What do you mean when you say, "the laws of Nature"?

– I mean the laws of Nature that Nature is revealing to us today, because out of all the elements in Nature, man is the most developed. It's necessary to understand that we exist within Nature and not above it. We submit to it. Therefore, we should study the laws of Nature and follow them. If we do, we will always be in a comfortable state and will feel good.

This enormous system permeates us with different forces. All of our thoughts and desires come from it. By "Nature," we refer to the system of forces that controls all of matter, energy, and information, everything—from subatomic particles through mammoth constellations, and beyond—and also the levels of Nature that we have not attained and that we hope to discover in the future.

The more we research Nature, the more it is revealed to us as integral, a single whole. And therefore, the integral approach to the world is becoming truly sought after.

– Can you give an example of one of the laws of Nature?

– The law of the universal interaction of all the forces, all the laws, all the elements of Nature. In Nature, they always exist in their total correspondence.

This system contains myriad equations with innumerable changing parameters, and they must all be brought to unity with each other, to a single integral whole.

These equations contain one main unknown, one parameter—man—who has been given freedom of will and can willingly or coercively participate in the act of bringing everything in existence to the common integral whole.

Today, humanity is still pondering whether or not it should join this integral unification of Nature, which Nature is starting to realize in our time. We have to join the system of Nature consciously, voluntarily, independently, by moving together with Nature. That is how we will learn from Nature. We will attain this unification conjointly, in a coordinated fashion. By understanding it, we will create a different society and different relationships among us.

We will understand what the integral Nature is and how it works. We will see the whole system and will discover its concealed factors, which influence us but are still unknown today. We will be able to feel the deep, secret reason for everything that exists on our small planet and in the cosmos. We will discover the reasons for our inner states and the conditions for attaining absolute comfort—the causes of life and death, of all evolution, which are contained in Nature, and the common plan of Creation.

Astrophysicists feel the universe as a thought. And we will be able to discover that thought if we voluntarily "go for it," meaning without resisting it and without remaining small, miserable animals on the surface of our planet. If we desire to study in order to change ourselves, we will be able to truly understand the entire system of the universe and solve all these equations. This wonderful, enthralling idea will elevate us and the whole of humanity to the *human* level.

However, if we resist it, Nature will still bring us there, but it will do so by exerting pressure, through great suffering, whose beginning we are already beginning to sense. Then we will be forced to reduce our egoism, start gathering into groups, and learn to live together. It's well known that suffering brings people closer. Thus, through negative influences, and Nature has a lot of them in store for us on different levels, we will still be brought to a state where we will rise above our egoism and attain the right, integral interaction.

But the price will be tremendous: wars, suffering, and losses. And as a result, the relics of humanity that survive will still have to become similar to Nature.

WE ARE TALKING ABOUT SURVIVAL

- Most people have a practical, earthly mind. This kind of person will ask, "How can this affect me personally?"

- We are talking about the survival of each and every person. Ecologists, political scientists, and natural scientists all say that we are living on an overheated planet. We have practically drained its resources, and in the next 10-15 years nothing will be left of the natural wealth. It's not even wealth anymore. It is all in the past. Under the earth's surface, there is no more gold or silver for production, not to mention jewelry. There is no petroleum, gas, or rare metals, and there is a shortage of drinking water. We are talking about the average person's survival, while that person doesn't want to think about it.

He is not sufficiently developed to care about the fate of the world and humanity, and I understand that. We cannot condemn people. But we do have to condemn ourselves and discuss how it is possible to get through to that kind of person.

To the extent he will have to be included in this mechanism, we will have to convince him, teach him, and rear him so he can participate and understand—to the necessary degree—that by that he truly does great work and is saving himself.

We don't have to scare anyone, but we do have to tell people the truth about what is happening. We can't conceal it and shut our eyes to it. We can't keep up the "Eat, drink, and be merry" attitude. We must look at the world rationally. If there were no remedy, then all that were left would be to "party" ourselves to the end. But since *there is* a remedy, why move toward suffering when we can already be moving elsewhere? And this won't even cost us anything. We just have to pay attention to the interaction between us.

We will have to carry out the appeal to "Love your neighbor as yourself," which is common to all religions and to which no one objects. It's just that no one can actually do it. But Nature compels us to do just that.

– In what form and who can bring this information to the average person without scaring him off?

– The mass media should gradually start publishing this information in the proper form, guided by psychologists, sociologists, political scientists, and people who understand how to handle society. People have to be approached gently, without causing panic because that won't help.

The solution to this problem depends on each and every one of us, and all of us together. The problem is purely social, therefore the government cannot solve it by forceful actions, but only through explanation and upbringing. For that reason, the entire responsibility is incumbent upon sociologists, psychologists, and the mass media.

We are not scaring anyone or shouting, even though we are sensing an enormous wave, a tsunami that is coming our way. Problems with lacking clean drinking water, food shortages, problems with children, domestic issues, and generally, issues in all areas of human existence. They will only escalate, and all of this is caused only by our improper interaction with one another.

These problems have been brewing for a long time, but they were not so apparent to the average person. In the 1960s, the Club of Rome already warned about it. And today many international organizations are sounding the alarm but it has not yet reached the masses. And most important, the necessary measures to remedy the situation have not yet been implemented. We have to start implementing them, but without scaring anyone.

A BUNKER WON'T SAVE US FROM THE INTEGRAL "TSUNAMI"

– Today we are observing a new phenomenon that's happening on a massive scale: wealthy people are starting to buy up property in the mountains of Switzerland, buying houses somewhere out in the tundra. They feel that something is indeed about to happen, and have decided, "I will quickly run away and will wait it out in the mountains."

– This is the natural drive of any egoist: to pile up everything that's necessary somewhere in a bunker and wait out the war that will roll over the whole world. There, on the surface, the war will obliterate everything and once it's over, I will come out to the open. New birds will come out singing on new trees, on a new earth, and everything will be okay.

But that's impossible because the issue at stake is a change of paradigm for the entire human society, its inner state, people's relationships with one another. Each of us will have to internally correspond to the common field of Nature that demands integration from us.

If I sit in a bunker with everything prepared ahead of time, down to artificial climate for a thousand years (a person thinks he is immortal), I will still sense my opposition to the single, integral field because on the inside, I did not change myself to match it.

No bunker will help me. My animate body will still suffer. New conditions will arise that will destroy me, not letting me survive in any incubator or any shell because on the inside, by my parameters, aspirations, and qualities, I won't correspond to today's integral "tsunami" that is moving in on me. It is a wave to which we will have to correspond. If we do, we will ride it with pleasure, in nature's bosom. If we don't, it will wipe us off the face of the earth.

For the first time ever, we are encountering our discrepancy with Nature not on the physical level, but on the inner, psychological, mental, and moral level, and we have to attain that level. This is not a physical salvation, but an inner one.

We have to become similar to Nature not in the physical parameters, but by the inner, integral network of connections among us, which is coming down and pressing on our world. If we don't correspond to its form, it will simply destroy us.

FROM "ME" TO "WE"

– If I do correspond to it, will I be leading some miserable existence just to survive, or is there something good in store for us, better than what we have now?

– The state we will reach is one that cannot be surpassed by anything. It is a state in which all problems and conflicts are resolved, in which man attains the deepest levels of Nature and himself.

It is an expansion of man's mind, emotions, qualities, and senses through the bounds of the infinite Nature, where we include all the worlds, states, and dimensions that we currently neither understand nor feel. The integral connection between us has to bring us to that state.

And most important, once we are included in the general quality of all of Nature, we will begin to feel its eternity and perfection, and this sensation will become our lives. We have to rise from the state of "me" to the state of "we," which is infinite, eternal, and perfect. In that state, we will stop feeling our individuality and will perceive only our inclusion in others.

It's as if a person rises above the problem of life and death and starts to feel a higher level. He does not sympathize with the body, this animate state, but with the energy or information that is in the single field that includes all of us.

We really are included in a single field of energy, thoughts, mind, desires, and intentions. And this field is not within our bodies; it is what's between us, what connects us.

Within this field, you feel what I feel, another person thinks what I think, and so on.

Scientists have researched this topic, and learned that we are actually in one informational body. When we enter this level of interconnection, we begin sensing ourselves as not living the animate life (the life of our body), but the life of this information, the single communication. And then a person feels that he doesn't sympathize with his animate life, but with the eternal, perfect life.

Therein lies nature's program: to bring our inner component, called "human," which differentiates us from the animate level, to its true form or true level—total interaction within the sensation of eternity and perfection of the whole of Nature.

THE NECESSITY TO CREATE A GLOBAL ORGANIZATION

– Is this information field something alien within us, or do we simply have to reveal what is instilled inside of us?

– It is instilled inside of us. This ability was expressed in certain individuals throughout different times. They are people who aspire to this state, who wish to research it, to propagate it, and to somehow realize it.

They are the philosophers of the past, utopians, and in part, socialists. They are scientists, researchers, politicians, and businessmen. As we know, the core of the Club of Rome consisted of successful businessmen and politicians. These people are completely different, but as a rule, they are all educated and forward-thinking. They are people with a broad vision, who can rise above their personal interests and feel a certain inner pressure. Today there are many people in the world who are like that.

It is necessary to create a worldwide organization that will include all of these people regardless of origin or political and social convictions so they can get together, develop a single system of integral upbringing, and offer it to the world.

Our organization is working on it, and we would like to collaborate with anyone who supports this thought. We pose no preconditions.

– You said that we will have to realize the principles of integrality in practice over the next 10 years. What specifically should we do, and how can we begin to realize what you describe?

– The realization has to happen along several channels. We have to consider the mentality of each group in the population and approach each of them differently, considering the type of activities they do and their age. We have to involve all mass media systems, gradually developing them and holding daily seminars at people's work places. The non-working people will have to visit special events and clubs where they can study. It will be like a worldwide university where every person on earth has to take this type of course for becoming a "new human being," telling him in simple terms about everything we talked about. It's also necessary to participate in all kinds of practical studies.

Half of our school hours should be devoted to such studies. It has to become the most important thing in society. This idea must permeate every person from all directions using communication, connection, interaction, and mutual help. But first, a person must be internally disposed to it. We have to gradually reconstruct the entire system.

Industry and production have to be reformed because we are disparate from Nature not only in our thoughts, but also on the material level. We have to shift to reasonable consumption, taking from the earth only what we need for existence. We don't have to exist in a restricted manner, but on the level of a normal person's consumption, and not beyond. That is how we will be merciful to "mother earth."

We have to teach people. Gradually, through school, work, TV, and internet, everyone will begin to understand what integrality means. Everything must work toward our objective: survival.

NO DISCOUNTS FOR AGE

– What should this course consist of? And who should teach it?

– We have to prepare many educators and instructors, although in today's conditions lessons can be held virtually as well.

A screen is turned on at a corporation, people enter a room, sit down, and start watching films, participating in games and discussions. And through the internet, the broadcast could be relayed to the whole planet.

But alongside it, it's necessary to prepare people. An educator is the most in-demand profession today.

We have always worked on education, but now we have to look at education differently and work in the direction of upbringing, on morally raising man to the "human" level. This requires joint efforts.

When you explain to a person that there is no other way to go and this is the necessity of today, he starts to understand it, although of course, it doesn't happen right away. Then, by the united efforts of our organization and many others that act in the same direction, we will be able to do this. We don't have any other choice.

– How should a meeting happen between a specialist on integral upbringing and say, an interested CEO of a corporation?

– I don't think this should require the agreement of the CEO. Everything has to happen under the auspices of the UN and UNESCO, which will give out policies and orders to all the governments. And every government will make the laws regarding changes in the workday, in the study process at schools, and so on.

No one is exempt from inclusion in this system. Pensioners do not receive a pension unless their pension books say that they have taken this course. There are no discounts for age!

Today the elderly have to be drawn to this process according to their ability, since we become included in it with our desires to be in the right connection with one another, therefore age doesn't matter. Everyone fits into this system.

Anyone living on this planet has to aspire to this state. That way, we will elicit sympathy from Nature, its positive response. This is why we are talking about the whole of humanity.

It will be necessary to create the appropriate databank: briefings, lectures, discussions, and talks using all sorts of films, clips, and so on. It has to be checked and gradually inculcated into practice, bringing the information to the population.

It will be necessary to have an enormous army of educators who will visit corporations. At learning establishments, the educators will constantly have to work together with the teachers.

It will be necessary to organize clubs, community centers, places where free consultations are given, interesting evenings are held, as well as panel games, meetings, and concerts. Everything must be done in the spirit of unity, teaching every person how to become included in this system internally, how to start feeling it, and most important, how to come closer to feeling this informational, sensual, rational network between us.

At the end of the day, we are all one, a single human image. How can I start feeling it? For that we have the rudiments of inner qualities, but we have to develop them.

As soon as people begin to feel it, they will instinctively start acting conjointly. The network will begin to live within them and control them, and they will willingly, happily follow this common direction. Then we will discover a humanity that is interconnected into one, healthy organism.

THE LANGUAGE OF INNER CONTACT

– How will this connection manifest?

– People still don't feel the inner connection between them, which means that we have to show which actions are the most appropriate. We cannot show the right inner actions, but they can manifest in some way on the outside.

For example, I give someone a gift, thus externally expressing my inner feelings. As a psychologist, you understand very well when the internality and the externality match or don't match. This is important in children's upbringing in order for them to understand you correctly. Thus, using speech and body language, we will develop the language of inner contacts among us.

When we really come into this contact, we won't need computers or the internet. We will have interpersonal contact on the level of informational, sensual, and rational fields, and we will rise to a level where our thoughts and desires are in perpetual contact. That is where we have to create a commonality called "the new humanity."

A person can be brought to this through various external exercises such as games, panel games, discussions, conversations, large open sites for such actions, films, concerts, and theatre shows.

Any external forms of expression that people have created in order to express their inner essence may be used. We just have to add these forms of expression to the new urge, the inner impulse.

Finally, writers, playwrights, and scriptwriters will have productive ideas and infinite possibilities for being creative.

INTEGRAL IDEAS FOR THE CREATIVE ARTS

- I have a friend who's a filmmaker and screenwriter. What should I suggest to him? What should the script be about, and how should it be built to contain integral ideas?

- It's necessary to write about a person who really desires to understand what the integral nature is, about his psychological, inner problems of interacting with himself. Describe his problems with the people around him, how he is trying to do something but they don't understand why he acts as he does. Talk about their attempts to enter this system, the impossibility to succeed, how it is expressed, and so on. Talk about the problems between children and parents, how they are resolved, and man's interaction with Nature. But mainly, it should be about a person's relations with himself and with the environment. All pieces of art and culture are built on those relations.

We are giving creative people an idea that they are obligated to start realizing as citizens of the world, by creating art that explains our situation in the new world.

We have many such ideas. But as usual we lack the resources and the performers to execute them. But we are open to creative people and will be happy to share our ideas with them about how it is possible to present this new state, sensation, and worldview on different levels.

All the eternal topics such as love and hate, human conflicts, and everything else can be depicted in this vein, and it will really be useful for everyone.

– Does that mean that we present a dramatic situation, and at the end the people involved have to reach an agreement?

– Not necessarily. But they do have to discern certain elements of the integral society. There doesn't necessarily have to be a "happy end." We are realists and do not want to stuff people with unrealistic illusions.

It has to be an action that's very close to life, a demonstration of our urgent problems and their possible solutions. But mainly, it's not about their decisions but about their agreement or lack of it, and how it happens with different people, in their connections with others, in various conflicts.

– When we talked about children, we noted that it's very important for a child to understand that every action he makes is reflected in the people around him. Is this what you mean?

– Yes. After all, human society is an extremely powerful amplifier of my thoughts and feelings. Whatever influence I have on society with my thoughts and feelings, that is how this system automatically reflects everything back to me.

Human society is absolute and perfect in relation to each of us. The only imperfect person is me because of my incorrect, non-integral inclusion in it.

I am like a part of an electronic network or scheme that is dysfunctional in some regard. I was created this way. And I

264 THE PSYCHOLOGY OF THE INTEGRAL SOCIETY

am included in this system, but I don't work in a coordinated fashion with it. And to the extent I bring interferences into it, the system multiplies my interferences. Because I agitate it and force it to be unbalanced, these flaws return to me. Can you imagine how my transgressions are augmented? Billions of times over!

They become expressed in me through illnesses, family problems, problems with my children, and in business. Suddenly my bank goes bankrupt or something happens at my corporation.

I am like a tiny bug in this system. The entire system consists of lots of little bugs like me and we are all connected with absolutely all of humanity on all levels. This proper interaction must be shown.

When a person sees this, he experiences a purely egoistic desire to protect himself from the reverse negative connection that he cannot escape. You are in it and are plugged into it, and you can't go anywhere. If you make a 1 Volt error in it, the blow that will come back to you will be 1,000 Volts.

Practically, this is the state we are approaching. Putting it mildly, Nature is placing a very challenging task before us.

– I introduce a certain interference into the system and receive a response only once everything has calmed down. That is, I don't see the connection between the cause and the effect. Is this the problem?

– But you cannot blame anyone for anything. You are in an ideal system. It is ideal in relation to you and in relation to every person. You receive a negative feedback from it, which pressures you to look inside you so you can become included in the scheme correctlyThis reaction from Nature is not there to hurt you, but to correct you, to show you that you are not in agreement with the system yet.

THE FEMALE DESIRE WILL CORRECT EVERYTHING

– What specifically can and should a woman who has heard you and understood you do? Usually a woman goes and immediately tries to "fix" her husband.

– As a psychologist, you have located the correct point of influence—the woman. In fact, this is correct because in our learning system, if we tell a woman about the bright prospects for humanity, she will arrange the rest. The female desire and pressure will correct everything. A man is far more passive in this regard. But a woman has such an influence on her children and husband that it will force them to work on self-correction.

Thus, first of all, the emphasis should be on educating the female part of the planet's population because it is very receptive to it. It is necessary to find the right approach to women, the right connection with them, and to awaken their interest. This will give us entry into the educational program.

No one is slighting the other parts of the population here. But as we see, if a woman wants something, others around her start to gradually fall under her influence.

– Say a woman who has just finished watching our program meets her husband in the evening. What should she do? How should she start realizing this idea?

– How does she usually influence her husband? We understand that at the end of the day, whether he desires it or not, in a sense, a man is subjugated to his woman. This is Nature, and we shouldn't be embarrassed about it!

Every man sees his wife as a mother in some respect and is somewhat afraid of her, like a boy, even though he is already a grown man or even beyond. It comes from Nature. A woman gives life. She nurtures you, guides you, and rears you. In the end, everything you have today is what she has done. Even though we are talking about the importance of the father's role for a child, he is still behind the mother. She is everything to a child.

– Should she somehow motivate him to make these "integral actions"? What is the first step?

– The first step is for a woman to want it. Her desire is enough even without saying a single word. Don't you know how women do this?

– Yes, of course.

– That's how she elicits a feeling in a man. And with children, she will talk to them, and they will also receive the new, integral upbringing at school. The husband will also receive it at work or any other place he might be. But with her silent question, which drills right through the male part of the family, a woman definitely heightens and sharpens their sensation that this is important.

The male part does not have this sensation of importance. Its specifically the woman who truly cares and worries about the future.

If she becomes concerned about the future, then everyone else will start spinning around it as well. A man will realize the female desire. He does it in life anyway, in the egoistic form. And the right desires will be realized here, as well.

LET'S UNITE

– What would you wish to people who are already willing to become part of this system?

– I recommend to all of our viewers to try to understand how we can improve our lives.

We have already entered the period of great crises. But the truth is concealed from us and we are told that the crisis has passed. Yet the people who work in this area understand that nothing has passed. By concealing it, it's as if we are accumulating radioactive waste, which is starting to burn on the inside, ready to explode.

We don't have to conceal it. Let's open up and start clearing up this egoistic system! It is ruining us, and it is not leaving us practically any chance to lead a normal life. On the inside, we are constantly on the defense against one another, pushing each other away, belligerent and hostile. No one knows what future is in store for our children. Let's unite and hear what Nature has in store for us!

In reality, Nature is a mother and is treating us with care.

Today we are witnessing the first alarms of our discrepancies with Nature. These are the crises that are occurring. This works like any common system: When I cause a small disturbance to it, it responds back with a multiplex amplification of the disturbance that I caused in it, according to the principle of a negative feedback. But this is done deliberately to lead me to the right path.

We have a specific goal to achieve. We have to see the right direction in all of nature's negative reverberations. Let's study its language, and we will see its path, the program along which it is leading us. The deviations are caused by us, while Nature is trying to put us back on track through the feedback of different kinds of suffering. These sufferings are all correct and compulsory from Nature's end. However, when we begin to understand Nature's inner workings, we will attain eternity and perfection.

Let's all be convinced that there really is a wonderful future ahead of us, because there is, and let's bring our children there!

FURTHER READING

To help you determine which book you would like to read next, we have divided the books into six categories—Beginners, Intermediate, Advanced, Good for All, Textbooks, and For Children. The first three categories are divided by the level of prior knowledge readers are required to have in order to easily relate to the book. The Beginners Category requires no prior knowledge. The Intermediate Category requires reading one or two beginners' books first; and the Advanced level requires one or two books of each of the previous categories. The fourth category, Good for All, includes books you can always enjoy, whether you are a complete novice or well versed in Kabbalah.

The fifth category—Textbooks—includes translations of authentic source materials from earlier Kabbalists, such as the Ari, Rav Yehuda Ashlag (Baal HaSulam) and his son and successor, Rav Baruch Ashlag (the Rabash). As its name implies, the sixth category—For Children—includes books that are suitable for children ages 3 and above. Those are not Kabbalah books per se, but are rather inspired by the teaching and convey the Kabbalistic message of love and unity.

Additional material that has not yet been published can be found at www.kabbalah.info. All materials on this site, including e-versions of published books, can be downloaded free of charge directly from the store at www.kabbalahbooks.info.

BEGINNERS

The Spiritual Roots of the Holy Land

The Spiritual Roots of the Holy Land takes you on a wondrous journey through the land of Israel. As you take in the breathtaking pictures of the holy land, another layer of the age-old country is revealed—its spiritual roots, the ebb and flow of forces that have shaped the curvy landscape that is sacred to billions of people around the world. At the end of the book, you'll find roadmaps of Israel, to help you locate each place you visit, whether in mind or in body, and more details on the forefathers who have made this land the focal point of an entire planet.

Self-Interest vs. Altruism in the Global Era: How society can turn self-interests into mutual benefit

Self-Interest vs. Altruism in the Global Era presents a new perspective on the world's challenges, regarding them as necessary consequences of humanity's growing egotism, rather than a series of errors. In that spirit, the book suggests ways to *use* our egos for society's benefit, rather than trying to suppress them.

The earlier chapters offer a novel understanding of Creation in general, and of humanity's existence on this planet, in particular. Then, we are offered a birds-eye view of history as a record of humankind's growing egotism. The final chapters address our current social and political challenges, and explain how we can use our egos to resolve them, rather than letting them ruin our collective home, as we have done so many times before.

A Guide to the Hidden Wisdom of Kabbalah

A Guide to the Hidden Wisdom of Kabbalah is a light and reader-friendly guide to beginners in Kabbalah, covering everything from the history of Kabbalah to how this wisdom can help resolve the world crisis.

The book is set up in three parts: Part 1 covers the history, facts, and fallacies about Kabbalah, and introduces its key concepts. Part 2 tells you all about the spiritual worlds and other neat stuff like the meaning of letters and the power of music. Part 3 covers the implementation of Kabbalah at a time of world crisis.

Kabbalah Revealed: A Guide to a More Peaceful Life

This is the most clearly written, reader-friendly guide to making sense of the surrounding world. Each of its six chapters focuses on a different aspect of the wisdom of Kabbalah, illuminating its teachings and explaining them using various examples from our day-to-day lives.

The first three chapters in *Kabbalah Revealed* explain why the world is in a state of crisis, how our growing desires promote progress as well as alienation, and why the biggest deterrent to achieving positive change is rooted in our own spirits. Chapters Four through Six offer a prescription for positive change. In these chapters, we learn how we can use our spirits to build a personally peaceful life in harmony with all of Creation.

Wondrous Wisdom

This book offers an initial course on Kabbalah. Like all the books presented here, *Wondrous Wisdom* is based solely on authentic teachings passed down from Kabbalist teacher to student over thousands of years. At the heart of the book is a sequence of lessons revealing the nature of Kabbalah's wisdom and explaining how to attain it. For every person questioning "Who am I really?" and "Why am I on this planet?" this book is a must.

Awakening to Kabbalah: The Guiding Light of Spiritual Fulfillment

A distinctive, personal, and awe-filled introduction to an ancient wisdom tradition. In this book, Rav Laitman offers a deeper

272   THE PSYCHOLOGY OF THE INTEGRAL SOCIETY

understanding of the fundamental teachings of Kabbalah, and how you can use its wisdom to clarify your relationship with others and the world around you.

Using language both scientific and poetic, he probes the most profound questions of spirituality and existence. This provocative, unique guide will inspire and invigorate you to see beyond the world as it is and the limitations of your everyday life, become closer to the Creator, and reach new depths of the soul.

Kabbalah, Science, and the Meaning of Life

Science explains the mechanisms that sustain life; Kabbalah explains why life exists. In *Kabbalah, Science, and the Meaning of Life*, Rav Laitman combines science and spirituality in a captivating dialogue that reveals life's meaning.

For thousands of years Kabbalists have been writing that the world is a single entity divided into separate beings. Today the cutting-edge science of quantum physics states a very similar idea: that at the most fundamental level of matter, we are all literally one.

Science proves that reality is affected by the observer who examines it; and so does Kabbalah. But Kabbalah makes an even bolder statement: even the Creator, the Maker of reality, is within the observer. In other words, God is inside of us; He doesn't exist anywhere else. When we pass away, so does He.

These earthshaking concepts and more are eloquently introduced so that even readers new to Kabbalah or science will easily understand them. Therefore, if you're just a little curious about why you are here, what life means, and what you can do to enjoy it more, this book is for you.

From Chaos to Harmony

Many researchers and scientists agree that the ego is the reason behind the perilous state our world is in today. Laitman's groundbreaking book not only demonstrates that egoism has been the basis for all suffering throughout human history, but also shows how we can turn our plight to pleasure.

The book contains a clear analysis of the human soul and its problems, and provides a "roadmap" of what we need to do to once again be happy. *From Chaos to Harmony* explains how we can rise to a new level of existence on personal, social, national, and international levels.

Kabbalah for Beginners

Kabbalah for Beginners is a book for all those seeking answers to life's essential questions. We all want to know why we are here, why there is pain, and how we can make life more enjoyable. The four parts of this book provide us with reliable answers to these questions, as well as clear explanations of the gist of Kabbalah and its practical implementations.

Part One discusses the discovery of the wisdom of Kabbalah, and how it was developed, and finally concealed until our time. Part Two introduces the gist of the wisdom of Kabbalah, using ten easy drawings to help us understand the structure of the spiritual worlds, and how they relate to our world. Part Three reveals Kabbalistic concepts that are largely unknown to the public, and Part Four elaborates on practical means you and I can take, to make our lives better and more enjoyable for us and for our children.

INTERMEDIATE

The Kabbalah Experience

The depth of the wisdom revealed in the questions and answers within this book will inspire readers to reflect and contemplate. This is not a book to race through, but rather one that should be read thoughtfully and carefully. With this approach, readers will begin to experience a growing sense of enlightenment while simply absorbing the answers to the questions every Kabbalah student asks along the way.

The *Kabbalah Experience* is a guide from the past to the future, revealing situations that all students of Kabbalah will experience at some point along their journeys. For those who cherish every moment in life, this book offers unparalleled insights into the timeless wisdom of Kabbalah.

The Path of Kabbalah

This unique book combines beginners' material with more advanced concepts and teachings. If you have read a book or two of Laitman's, you will find this book very easy to relate to.

While touching upon basic concepts such as perception of reality and Freedom of Choice, *The Path of Kabbalah* goes deeper and expands beyond the scope of beginners' books. The structure of the worlds, for example, is explained in greater detail here than in the "pure" beginners' books. Also described is the spiritual root of mundane matters such as the Hebrew calendar and the holidays.

ADVANCED

The Science of Kabbalah

Kabbalist and scientist Rav Michael Laitman, PhD, designed this book to introduce readers to the special language and terminology of the authentic wisdom of Kabbalah. Here, Rav Laitman reveals authentic Kabbalah in a manner both rational and mature. Readers are gradually led to understand the logical design of the Universe and the life that exists in it.

The Science of Kabbalah, a revolutionary work unmatched in its clarity, depth, and appeal to the intellect, will enable readers to approach the more technical works of Baal HaSulam (Rabbi

Yehuda Ashlag), such as *The Study of the Ten Sefirot* and *The Book of Zohar*. Readers of this book will enjoy the satisfying answers to the riddles of life that only authentic Kabbalah provides. Travel through the pages and prepare for an astonishing journey into the Upper Worlds.

Introduction to the Book of Zohar

This volume, along with *The Science of Kabbalah*, is a required preparation for those who wish to understand the hidden message of *The Book of Zohar*. Among the many helpful topics dealt with in this text is an introduction to the "language of roots and branches," without which the stories in *The Zohar* are mere fable and legend. *Introduction to the Book of Zohar* will provide readers with the necessary tools to understand authentic Kabbalah as it was originally meant to be—as a means to attain the Upper Worlds.

The Book of Zohar: annotations to the Ashlag commentary

The Book of Zohar (*The Book of Radiance*) is an age-old source of wisdom and the basis for all Kabbalistic literature. Since its appearance nearly 2,000 years ago, it has been the primary, and often only, source used by Kabbalists.

For centuries, Kabbalah was hidden from the public, which was deemed not yet ready to receive it. However, our generation has been designated by Kabbalists as the first generation that *is* ready to grasp the concepts in *The Zohar*. Now we can put these principles into practice in our lives.

Written in a unique and metaphorical language, *The Book of Zohar* enriches our understanding of reality and widens our worldview. Although the text deals with one subject only—how to relate to the Creator—it approaches it from different angles. This allows each of us to find the particular phrase or word that will carry us into the depths of this profound and timeless wisdom.

GOOD FOR ALL

The Point in the Heart: A Source of Delight for My Soul

The Point in the Heart; a Source of Delight for My Soul is a unique collection of excerpts from a man whose wisdom has earned him devoted students in North America and the world over. Michael Laitman is a scientist, a Kabbalist, and a great thinker who presents ancient wisdom in a compelling style.

This book does not profess to teach Kabbalah, but rather gently introduces ideas from the teaching. The Point in the Heart is a window to a new perception. As the author himself testifies to the wisdom of Kabbalah, "It is a science of emotion, a science of pleasure. You are welcome to open and to taste."

Attaining the Worlds Beyond

From the introduction to Attaining the Worlds Beyond: "...Not feeling well on the Jewish New Year's Eve of September 1991, my teacher called me to his bedside and handed me his notebook, saying, 'Take it and learn from it.' The following morning, he perished in my arms, leaving me and many of his other disciples without guidance in this world.

"He used to say, 'I want to teach you to turn to the Creator, rather than to me, because He is the only strength, the only Source of all that exists, the only one who can really help you, and He awaits your prayers for help. When you seek help in your search for freedom from the bondage of this world, help in elevating yourself above this world, help in finding the self, and help in determining your purpose in life, you must turn to the Creator, who sends you all those aspirations in order to compel you to turn to Him.'"

Attaining the Worlds Beyond holds within it the content of that notebook, as well as other inspiring texts. This book reaches out to all those seekers who want to find a logical, reliable way to understand the world's phenomena. This fascinating introduction to the wisdom of Kabbalah will enlighten the mind, invigorate the heart, and move readers to the depths of their souls.

Bail Yourself Out

In *Bail Yourself Out: how you can emerge strong from the world crisis*, Laitman introduces several extraordinary concepts that weave into a complete solution: 1) The crisis is essentially not financial, but *psychological*: People have stopped trusting each other, and where there is no trust there is no trade, but only war, isolation, and pain. 2) This mistrust is a result of a *natural process* that's been evolving for millennia and is culminating today. 3) To resolve the crisis, we must first *understand* the process that created the alienation. 4) The first, and most important, step to understanding the crisis is to *inform* people about this natural process through books, such as *Bail Yourself Out*, TV, cinema, and any other means of communication. 5) With this information, we will "*revamp*" our relationships and build them on trust, collaboration, and most importantly, care. This mending process will guarantee that we and our families will prosper in a world of plenty.

Basic Concepts in Kabbalah

This is a book to help readers cultivate an *approach to the concepts* of Kabbalah, to spiritual objects, and to spiritual terms. By reading and re-reading in this book, one develops internal observations, senses, and approaches that did not previously exist within. These newly acquired observations are like sensors that "feel" the space around us that is hidden from our ordinary senses.

Hence, *Basic Concepts in Kabbalah* is intended to foster the contemplation of spiritual terms. Once we are integrated with these terms, we can begin to see, with our inner vision, the unveiling of the spiritual structure that surrounds us, almost as if a mist has been lifted.

This book is not aimed at the study of facts. Instead, it is a book for those who wish to awaken the deepest and subtlest sensations they can possess.

Children of Tomorrow:
Guidelines for Raising Happy Children in the 21st Century

Children of Tomorrow is a new beginning for you and your children. Imagine being able to hit the reboot button and get it right this time. No hassle, no stress, and best of all—no guessing.

The big revelation is that raising kids is all about games and play, relating to them as small grownups, and making all major decisions together. You will be surprised to discover how teaching kids about positive things like friendship and caring for others automatically spills into other areas of our lives through the day.

Open any page and you will find thought-provoking quotes about every aspect of children's lives: parent-children relations, friendships and conflicts, and a clear picture of how schools should be designed and function. This book offers a fresh perspective on how to raise our children, with the goal being the happiness of all children everywhere.

The Wise Heart:
Tales and allegories by three contemporary sages

"Our inner work is to tune our hearts and our senses to perceive the spiritual world," says Michael Laitman in the poem Spiritual Wave. *The Wise Heart* is a lovingly crafted anthology comprised of tales and allegories by Kabbalist Dr. Michael Laitman, his mentor, Rav Baruch Ashlag (Rabash), and Rabash's father and mentor, Rav Yehuda Ashlag, author of the acclaimed *Sulam* (Ladder) commentary on *The Book of Zohar*.

Kabbalah students and enthusiasts in Kabbalah often wonder what the spiritual world actually feels like to a Kabbalist. The allegories in this delicate compilation provide a glimpse into those feelings.

The poems herein are excerpts from letters and lessons given by these three spiritual giants to their students through the years. They offer surprising and often amusing depictions of human nature, with a loving and tender touch that is truly unique to Kabbalists. Indeed, *The Wise Heart* is a gift of wisdom and delight for any wisdom seeking heart.

TEXTBOOKS

Shamati (I Heard)

Rav Michael Laitman's words on the book: Among all the texts and notes that were used by my teacher, Rav Baruch Shalom Halevi Ashlag (the Rabash), there was one special notebook he always carried. This notebook contained the transcripts of his conversations with his father, Rav Yehuda Leib Halevi Ashlag (Baal HaSulam), author of the *Sulam* (Ladder) commentary on *The Book of Zohar*, *The Study of the Ten Sefirot* (a commentary on the texts of the Kabbalist, Ari), and of many other works on Kabbalah.

Not feeling well on the Jewish New Year's Eve of September 1991, the Rabash summoned me to his bedside and handed me a notebook, whose cover contained only one word, *Shamati* (I Heard). As he handed the notebook, he said, "Take it and learn from it." The following morning, my teacher perished in my arms, leaving me and many of his other disciples without guidance in this world.

Committed to Rabash's legacy to disseminate the wisdom of Kabbalah, I published the notebook just as it was written, thus retaining the text's transforming powers. Among all the books of Kabbalah, *Shamati* is a unique and compelling creation.

Kabbalah for the Student

Kabbalah for the Student offers authentic texts by Rav Yehuda Ashlag, author of the *Sulam* (Ladder) commentary on *The Book of Zohar*, his son and successor, Rav Baruch Ashlag, as well as other great Kabbalists. It also offers illustrations that accurately depict the evolution of the Upper Worlds as Kabbalists experience them. The book also contains several explanatory essays that help us understand the texts within.

In *Kabbalah for the Student*, Rav Michael Laitman, PhD, Rav Baruch Ashlag's personal assistant and prime student, compiled all the texts a Kabbalah student would need in order to attain the spiritual worlds. In his daily lessons, Rav Laitman bases his teaching on these inspiring texts, thus helping novices and veterans alike to better understand the spiritual path we undertake on our fascinating journey to the Higher Realms.

Rabash—the Social Writings

Rav Baruch Shalom HaLevi Ashlag (Rabash) played a remarkable role in the history of Kabbalah. He provided us with the necessary final link connecting the wisdom of Kabbalah to our human experience. His father and teacher was the great Kabbalist, Rav Yehuda Leib HaLevi Ashlag, known as Baal HaSulam for his *Sulam* (Ladder) commentary on *The Book of Zohar*. Yet, if not for the essays of Rabash, his father's efforts to disclose the wisdom of Kabbalah to all would have been in vain. Without those essays, few would be able to achieve the spiritual attainment that Baal HaSulam so desperately wanted us to obtain.

The writings in this book aren't just for reading. They are more like an experiential user's guide. It is very important to work with them in order to see what they truly contain. The reader should try to put them into practice by living out the emotions Rabash so masterfully describes. He always advised his students to summarize the articles, to work with the texts, and those who attempt it discover that it always yields new insights. Thus, readers are advised to work with the texts, summarize them, translate them, and implement them in the group. Those who do so will discover the power in the writings of Rabash.

Gems of Wisdom:
words of the great Kabbalists from all generations

Through the millennia, Kabbalists have bequeathed us with numerous writings. In their compositions, they have laid out a structured method that can lead, step by step, unto a world of eternity and wholeness.

Gems of wisdom is a collection of selected excerpts from the writings of the greatest Kabbalists from all generations, with particular emphasis on the writings of Rav Yehuda Leib HaLevi Ashlag (Baal HaSulam), author of the Sulam [Ladder] commentary of The Book of Zohar.

The sections have been arranged by topics, to provide the broadest view possible on each topic. This book is a useful guide to any person desiring spiritual advancement.

FOR CHILDREN

Together Forever:
The story about the magician who didn't want to be alone

On the surface, Together Forever is a children's story. But like all good children's stories, it transcends boundaries of age, culture, and upbringing.

In *Together Forever*, the author tells us that if we are patient and endure the trials we encounter along our life's path, we will become stronger, braver, and wiser. Instead of growing weaker, we will learn to create our own magic and our own wonders as only a magician can.

In this warm, tender tale, Michael Laitman shares with children and parents alike some of the gems and charms of the spiritual world. The wisdom of Kabbalah is filled with spellbinding stories. *Together Forever* is yet another gift from this ageless source of wisdom, whose lessons make our lives richer, easier, and far more fulfilling.

Miracles Can Happen: Tales for children, but not only...

"Miracles Can Happen," Princes Peony," and "Mary and the Paints" are only three of ten beautiful stories for children ages 3-10. Written especially for children, these short tales convey a single message of love, unity, and care for all beings. The unique illustrations were carefully crafted to contribute to the overall message of the book, and a child who's heard or read any story in this collection is guaranteed to go to sleep smiling.

The Baobab that Opened Its Heart: and Other Nature Tales for Children

The Baobab that Opened Its Heart is a collection of stories for children, but not just for them. The stories in this collection were written with the love of Nature, of people, and specifically with children in mind. They all share the desire to tell nature's tale of unity, connectedness, and love.

Kabbalah teaches that love is nature's guiding force, the reason for creation. The stories in this book convey it in the unique way that Kabbalah engenders in its students. The variety of authors and diversity of styles allows each reader to find the story that they like most.

ABOUT BNEI BARUCH

Bnei Baruch is an international group of Kabbalists who share the wisdom of Kabbalah with the entire world. The study materials (in over 30 languages) are authentic Kabbalah texts that were passed down from generation to generation.

HISTORY AND ORIGIN

In 1991, following the passing of his teacher, Rav Baruch Shalom HaLevi Ashlag (The Rabash), Michael Laitman, Professor of Ontology and the Theory of Knowledge, PhD in Philosophy and Kabbalah, and MS in Medical Bio-Cybernetics, established a Kabbalah study group called "Bnei Baruch." He called it Bnei Baruch (Sons of Baruch) to commemorate his mentor, whose side he never left in the final twelve years of his life, from 1979 to 1991. Dr. Laitman had been Ashlag's prime student and personal assistant, and is recognized as the successor to Rabash's teaching method.

The Rabash was the firstborn son and successor of Rav Yehuda Leib HaLevi Ashlag, the greatest Kabbalist of the 20th century. Rav Ashlag authored the most authoritative and comprehensive commentary on *The Book of Zohar*, titled *The Sulam* (Ladder) *Commentary*. He was the first to reveal the complete method for spiritual ascent, and thus was known as Baal HaSulam (Owner of the Ladder).

Bnei Baruch bases its entire study method on the path paved by these two great spiritual leaders.

THE STUDY METHOD

The unique study method developed by Baal HaSulam and his son, the Rabash, is taught and applied on a daily basis by Bnei Baruch. This method relies on authentic Kabbalah sources such as *The Book of Zohar*, by Rabbi Shimon Bar-Yochai, *The Tree of Life*, by the Ari, and *The Study of the Ten Sefirot*, by Baal HaSulam.

While the study relies on authentic Kabbalah sources, it is carried out in simple language and uses a scientific, contemporary approach. The unique combination of an academic study method and personal experiences broadens the students' perspective and awards them a new perception of the reality they live in. Those on the spiritual path are thus given the necessary tools to study themselves and their surrounding reality.

Bnei Baruch is a diverse movement of tens of thousands of students worldwide. Students can choose their own paths and intensity of their studies according to their unique conditions and abilities.

THE MESSAGE

The essence of the message disseminated by Bnei Baruch is universal: unity of the people, unity of nations and love of man.

For millennia, Kabbalists have been teaching that love of man should be the foundation of all human relations. This love prevailed in the days of Abraham, Moses, and the group of Kabbalists that they established. If we make room for these seasoned, yet contemporary values, we will discover that we possess the power to put differences aside and unite.

The wisdom of Kabbalah, hidden for millennia, has been waiting for the time when we would be sufficiently developed and ready to implement its message. Now, it is emerging as a solution that can unite diverse factions everywhere, enabling us, as individuals and as a society, to meet today's challenges.

ACTIVITIES

Bnei Baruch was established on the premise that "only by expansion of the wisdom of Kabbalah to the public can we be awarded complete redemption" (Baal HaSulam). Therefore, Bnei Baruch offers a variety of ways for people to explore and discover the purpose of their lives, providing careful guidance for beginners and advanced students alike.

Internet

Bnei Baruch's international website, www.kab.info, presents the authentic wisdom of Kabbalah using essays, books, and original texts. It is by far the most expansive source of authentic Kabbalah material on the Internet, containing a unique, extensive library for readers to thoroughly explore the wisdom of Kabbalah. Additionally, the media archive, www.kabbalahmedia.info, contains thousands of media items, downloadable books, and a vast reservoir of texts, video and audio files in many languages.

Bnei Baruch's online Kabbalah Education Center offers free Kabbalah courses for beginners, initiating students into this profound body of knowledge in the comfort of their own homes.

Dr. Laitman's daily lessons are also aired live on www.kab.tv, along with complementary texts and diagrams.

All these services are provided free of charge.

Television

In Israel, Bnei Baruch established its own channel, no. 66 on both cable and satellite, which broadcasts 24/7 Kabbalah TV. The channel is also aired on the Internet at www.kab.tv. All broadcasts on the channel are free of charge. Programs are adapted for all levels, from complete beginners to the most advanced.

Conferences

Twice a year, students gather for a weekend of study and socializing at conferences in various locations in the U.S., as well as an annual convention in Israel. These gatherings provide a great setting for meeting like-minded people, for bonding, and for expanding one's understanding of the wisdom.

Kabbalah Books

Bnei Baruch publishes authentic books, written by Baal HaSulam, his son, the Rabash, as well as books by Dr. Michael Laitman. The books of Rav Ashlag and Rabash are essential for complete understanding of the teachings of authentic Kabbalah, explained in Laitman's lessons.

Dr. Laitman writes his books in a clear, contemporary style based on the key concepts of Baal HaSulam. These books are a vital link between today's readers and the original texts. All the books are available for sale, as well as for free download.

Paper

Kabbalah Today is a free paper produced and disseminated by Bnei Baruch in many languages, including English, Hebrew, Spanish, and Russian. It is apolitical, non-commercial, and written in a clear, contemporary style. The purpose of *Kabbalah Today* is to expose the vast knowledge hidden in the wisdom of Kabbalah at no cost and in a clear, engaging style for readers everywhere.

Kabbalah Lessons

As Kabbalists have been doing for centuries, Laitman gives a daily lesson. The lessons are given in Hebrew and are simultaneously interpreted into seven languages—English, Russian, Spanish, French, German, Italian, and Turkish—by skilled and experienced interpreters. As with everything else, the live broadcast is free of charge.

Funding

Bnei Baruch is a non-profit organization for teaching and sharing the wisdom of Kabbalah. To maintain its independence and purity of intentions, Bnei Baruch is not supported, funded, or otherwise tied to any government or political organization.

Since the bulk of its activity is provided free of charge, the prime sources of funding for the group's activities are donations and tithing—contributed by students on a voluntary basis—and Dr. Laitman's books, which are sold at cost.

HOW TO CONTACT BNEI BARUCH

1057 Steeles Avenue West, Suite 532
Toronto, ON, M2R 3X1
Canada

Bnei Baruch USA,
2009 85th street, #51,
Brooklyn, New York, 11214
USA

E-mail: info@kabbalah.info
Web site: www.kabbalah.info

Toll free in USA and Canada:
1-866-LAITMAN
Fax: 1-905 886 9697